Afghanistan's Local War

Building Local Defense Forces

Seth G. Jones, Arturo Muñoz

Prepared for the Marine Corps Intelligence Activity
Approved for public release; distribution unlimited

 NATIONAL DEFENSE RESEARCH INSTITUTE

The research described in this report was prepared for the Marine Corps Intelligence Activity. The research was conducted in the RAND National Defense Research Institute, a federally funded research and development center sponsored by the Office of the Secretary of Defense, the Joint Staff, the Unified Combatant Commands, the Department of the Navy, the Marine Corps, the defense agencies, and the defense Intelligence Community under Contract W74V8H-06-C-0002.

Library of Congress Control Number: 2010932125

ISBN: 978-0-8330-4988-9

Published 2010 by the RAND Corporation
1776 Main Street, P.O. Box 2138, Santa Monica, CA 90407-2138
1200 South Hayes Street, Arlington, VA 22202-5050
4570 Fifth Avenue, Suite 600, Pittsburgh, PA 15213-2665
RAND URL: http://www.rand.org/
To order RAND documents or to obtain additional information, contact
Distribution Services: Telephone: (310) 451-7002;
Fax: (310) 451-6915; Email: order@rand.org

Preface

This document examines the viability of establishing local defense forces in Afghanistan to complement Afghan National Security Forces. It focuses on security measures, especially on helping communities defend themselves against insurgent threats, rather than on broader economic, justice, and other development efforts. It concludes that local security forces are vital but should be small, defensive, under the immediate control of *jirgas* and *shuras*, and supported by national security forces. These conclusions are based on detailed research the authors conducted in Afghanistan and Pakistan, as well as on their examination of historical and anthropological work on tribal and community dynamics.

The research was sponsored by the Marine Corps Intelligence Activity and conducted within the Intelligence Policy Center of the RAND National Defense Research Institute, a federally funded research and development center sponsored by the Office of the Secretary of Defense, the Joint Staff, the Unified Combatant Commands, the Navy, the Marine Corps, the defense agencies, and the defense Intelligence Community.

For more information on RAND's Intelligence Policy Center, contact the Director, John Parachini. He can be reached by e-mail at John_Parachini@rand.org; by phone at 703-413-1100, extension 5579; or by mail at the RAND Corporation, 1200 South Hayes Street, Arlington, Virginia 22202-5050. More information about RAND is available at www.rand.org.

Contents

Figures and Table

Figures

Table

Executive Summary

Afghan and NATO officials have increasingly focused on protecting the local population as the linchpin of defeating the Taliban and other insurgent groups. Certain steps are important to achieving this objective, such as building competent Afghan national security forces, reintegrating insurgents, countering corruption, and improving governance. This document focuses on a complementary step: leveraging local communities, especially the use of traditional policing institutions, such as arbakai, chagha, and chalweshtai, to establish security and help mobilize rural Afghans against the Taliban and other insurgents.

Effectively leveraging local communities should significantly improve counterinsurgency prospects. Gaining the support of the population—especially mobilizing locals to fight insurgents, providing information on their locations and movements, and denying insurgent sanctuary in their areas—is the sine qua non of victory in counterinsurgency warfare. By tapping into tribes and other communities where grassroots resistance *already* exists, local defense forces can help mobilize communities simultaneously across multiple areas. The goal should be to help cause a "cascade" or "tip," in which momentum against the Taliban becomes unstoppable. In 2010, a growing number of communities in Kandahar, Helmand, Paktia, Herat, Paktika, Day Kundi, and other provinces mobilized and fought against insurgents. These cases present significant opportunities for counterinsurgency efforts in Afghanistan.

Successful efforts to protect the population need to include better understanding of local communities. Indeed, the Afghan and NATO governments often present the struggle as being between the Taliban and the central government in Kabul. But this dichotomy is false and is not likely to persuade rural villagers, who have never relied wholly on state institutions for law and order. Rural communities tend to be motivated by self-interest and self-sufficiency, preferring to secure their own villages rather than have outsiders do it for them. A failure to adopt an effective bottom-up effort will likely cripple counterinsurgency efforts. This analysis documents three lessons about the viability of establishing bottom-up security in Afghanistan.

First, security in Afghanistan has historically required a combination of top-down efforts from the central government and bottom-up efforts from local communities, as exemplified by Afghanistan's most recent stable period: the Musahiban dynasty (1929–1978). Since 2001, U.S. and broader international efforts have focused on establishing security from the top down through Afghan national security forces and other central government institutions. But history, anthropology, and counterinsurgency doctrine all indicate that local security forces are a critical complement to these national efforts.

Second, power in rural areas today remains local, and individuals generally identify themselves by their tribe, subtribe, clan, *qawm*, or community. A *qawm* is a unit of identification and solidarity that could be based on kinship, residence, or occupation. Pashtuns have historically used certain traditional institutions, such as arbakai and chalweshtai, to police their communities. These are not militias, as the term is often used in Afghanistan, which refer to large offensive forces under the command of warlords. Instead, they are defensive, village-level policing forces under the control of local shuras and jirgas, which are consultative councils.

Third, the Afghan government and NATO forces need to move quickly to establish a more-effective bottom-up strategy to complement top-down efforts by better leveraging local communities, especially in Pashtun areas. The Afghan government can work with existing community structures that oppose insurgents to establish village-level policing entities, with support from NATO countries when appropriate. Several steps are critical:

- Identify communities that have already (a) resisted the Taliban or other insurgent groups or (b) asked Afghan or NATO governments for assistance in resisting insurgents. Resistance needs to come from the grass roots. Many of these communities already have traditional policing structures, such as arbakai or chalweshtai.
- Ensure that the Afghan government takes the lead in training, mentoring, vetting, and overseeing local defense forces. The central government's role may be delicate, since some communities may not want a permanent central government presence in their villages.
- Utilize existing legitimate local institutions, such as jirgas and shuras, to exercise command and control of local defense forces, and use central government forces to provide oversight.
- Ensure that arbakai, chalweshtai, and other forces are small, village-level, and defensive. This will require regular coordination with Afghan national security forces. Some international forces may also need to live in—or near—villages to provide oversight and assistance.
- Establish a quick-reaction force composed of Afghan and NATO forces to support local defense forces that come under attack.
- Provide development aid that benefits the communities. It is essential to show the people concrete and sustainable benefits, particularly in the area of job creation.

There is a significant opportunity for mobilizing Afghans against the Taliban. Public opinion polls and other data indicate that the Taliban has failed to establish significant support among Afghans. The support bases of other groups, such as the Haqqani network and Gulbuddin Hekmatyar's Hezb-i-Islami, are even weaker. This reality presents an enormous window of opportunity that needs to be exploited. There are, of course, risks with any strategy, as this assessment documents. But the potential risks are outweighed by the potential gains, especially since Afghan and NATO forces can monitor and provide oversight to local defense forces and mitigate these risks.

Acknowledgments

This manuscript would not have been possible without the help of numerous individuals. David Phillips and Thomas Johnson provided helpful comments at a forum in Quantico, Virginia, on local defense forces. Michael Shurkin, Kathi Webb, and Adam Grissom reviewed the document; their critiques and suggestions were instrumental in clarifying points and filling in gaps. Ben Connable provided excellent information on civilian defense forces in other countries. Joya Laya and Sean Halpin provided helpful research assistance and helped shepherd the manuscript through production. We owe a special debt of gratitude to the government officials from the United States (including U.S. Special Operations Forces, the U.S. Marine Corps, U.S. Agency for International Development, and Department of State), Pakistan, Afghanistan, United Kingdom, and other countries who took time out of their busy schedules to provide information about local defense forces. Most did not want to be identified because of the sensitivity of the information they provided, so we have not thanked any of them by name.

Abbreviations

ANA	Afghan National Army
ANP	Afghan National Police
DDR	disarmament, demobilization, and reintegration
DIAG	disbandment of illegally armed groups
ISI	Pakistan's Directorate for Inter-Services Intelligence
NATO	North Atlantic Treaty Organization
NWFP	North West Frontier Province
SOF	Special Operations Forces

CHAPTER ONE

Introduction

In 2001, the United States led a successful insurgency against the Taliban government, reaching out to Tajik and Uzbek forces in northern and western Afghanistan, Hazara forces in the center, and Pashtun forces in the east and south. By 2002, however, the Taliban and other groups began to conduct initial offensive operations against NATO forces and the newly established Afghan government. The United States soon found itself in the unenviable position of waging a counterinsurgency. In barely a year, U.S. forces had shifted from operating as insurgents to counterinsurgents. By 2010, the insurgency had deepened. U.S. GEN Stanley McChrystal's assessment of Afghanistan noted that "we face not only a resilient and growing insurgency; there is also a crisis of confidence among Afghans—in both their government and the international community—that undermines our credibility and emboldens the insurgents."[1]

Among stated U.S. objectives in Afghanistan is facilitating Afghanistan's ability to govern itself. Governance is in part determined by the capabilities of local and national security forces to protect borders and respond to internal strife. However, Afghan history demonstrates that local security forces are important for establishing national security. This document examines the viability of establishing a bottom-up security strategy in Afghanistan to complement ongoing efforts at the national level. The focus here is on *security* measures, although economic and development efforts are clearly also key elements of a stable

---

[1] Stanley A. McChrystal, "COMISAF's Initial Assessment," memorandum to the Honorable Robert M. Gates, August 30, 2009, pp. 1-1.

nation and government. The overall success of any counterinsurgency campaign, of course, depends on a variety of interrelated factors.

In exploring a bottom-up strategy, we adopted several methodological approaches. First, we compiled a list of nearly two dozen tribal and other local policing cases dating from 1880 and briefly assessed their effectiveness. The results informed our analysis of local defense forces. Second, we met with dozens of tribal and community leaders across rural Afghanistan—especially the west, south, and east. We were particularly interested in gauging their views on several specific issues: the strength of tribes, subtribes, clans, and other social structures; the competence and strength of Afghan national security forces in their areas; the historical use of community policing structures, such as arbakai and chalweshtai; and the current status of these structures. Third, we examined the anthropological work on tribal and community dynamics.

For several reasons, there is a great deal of ignorance about power and politics in rural Afghanistan, especially in Pashtun areas affected by the insurgency. The first reason is selection bias. Few international civilians spend time in violent areas because of security concerns. Indeed, far too many U.S. and other NATO government officials are prohibited from traveling outside their bases or urban areas because of risk aversion. Most academics cannot access rural areas of the insurgency because it is too dangerous. Yet the insurgency is primarily a *rural* one. The increasing size of international bases in Kabul, Bagram, Kandahar, and other areas—including the traffic jams that we have personally experienced on several of these bases—is a testament to this risk aversion. It prevents foreigners from understanding rural Afghanistan and its inhabitants. Second, many foreigners, including government officials, project their Western views on Afghanistan. This bias has caused many foreigners, and even some Western-educated Afghan government officials, to look *only* to the central government for solutions. But security has required—and will continue to require—a combination of top-down and bottom-up efforts.

The rest of this document is divided as follows. Chapter Two outlines the debate between top-down and bottom-up models for Afghanistan, and examines the challenge of protecting the population. Chapter Three assesses the social structures in rural Afghanistan, especially the Pashtun areas in which the insurgency is primarily being waged. It also discusses some of the key policing institutions that Pashtuns and others have used to establish security in their villages. Chapter Four analyzes the effectiveness of local forces in Afghanistan and Pakistan since 1880. Chapter Five outlines a bottom-up security strategy and argues that local defense forces should be organized according to several key principles. Chapter Six discusses potential objections to the establishment of local forces and provides a brief conclusion.

CHAPTER TWO

The Challenge: Protecting the Population

Successful counterinsurgency requires protecting the local population and gaining its support—or at least acquiescence. Both insurgents and counterinsurgents need the support of the population to win. "The only territory you want to hold," one study concluded, "is the six inches between the ears of the *campesino*."[1] British General Sir Frank Kitson argued that the population is a critical element in counterinsurgency operations: "[T]his represents the water in which the fish swims."[2] Kitson borrowed the reference to the water and fish from one of the 20th century's most successful insurgents, Chinese leader Mao Tse-Tung. Mao wrote that there is an inextricable link in insurgencies "between the people and the troops. The former may be likened to water and the latter to the fish who inhabit it."[3]

One of the key challenges the U.S. military and other forces continue to face in Afghanistan is protecting the local population, especially in rural areas. As General McChrystal has argued, "Our strategy cannot be focused on seizing terrain or destroying insurgent forces;

[1] Daniel Siegel and Joy Hackel, "El Salvador: Counterinsurgency Revisited," in Michael T. Klare and Peter Kornbluh, eds., *Low Intensity Warfare: Counterinsurgency, Proinsurgency, and Antiterrorism in the Eighties*, New York: Pantheon Books, 1988, p. 119.

[2] Frank Kitson, *Low Intensity Operations: Subversion, Insurgency, Peacekeeping*, Hamden, Conn.: Archon Books, 1971, p. 49. On counterinsurgency strategies, also see Colonel C. E. Callwell, *Small Wars: Their Principles and Practice*, 3rd ed., Lincoln, Neb.: University of Nebraska Press, 1996, pp. 34–42; David Galula, *Counterinsurgency Warfare: Theory and Practice*, New York: Praeger, [1964] 2006, pp. 17–42.

[3] Mao Tse-Tung, *On Guerrilla Warfare*, tr. Samuel B. Griffith II, Urbana, Ill.: University of Illinois Press, 1961, p. 93.

our objective must be the population."[4] Indeed, a growing amount of research and field observations suggests that successful counterinsurgency requires improving governance and security for the local population.[5] As the U.S. Army and Marine Corps's Counterinsurgency Field Manual states,

> Progress in building support for the [host nation] government requires protecting the local populace. People who do not believe they are secure from insurgent intimidation, coercion, and reprisals will not risk overtly supporting [counterinsurgency] efforts.[6]

Since 2002, however, U.S. and other NATO efforts to establish security have largely focused on *national* security forces. This strategy should be only a piece of the overall counterinsurgency strategy. What is missing is partner forces working at the local level and reaching up.

Working from the Top Down

Since the Bonn agreement in December 2001, international efforts in Afghanistan have largely focused on top-down efforts to establish security by trying to strengthen central government institutions. On the security front, this has translated into building Afghan National Police (ANP) and Afghan National Army (ANA) forces as bulwarks against Taliban and other insurgent groups. On the economic and development fronts, it has translated into improving the central government's ability to deliver services to the population. As Ashraf Ghani, Afghanistan's former Minister of Finance, and Clare Lockhart argue, stability

---

4   McChrystal, "COMISAF's Initial Assessment." Also see, for example, Headquarters International Security Assistance Force, "ISAF Commander's Counterinsurgency Guidance," Kabul, 2009.

5   See, for example, James D. Fearon and David D. Laitin, "Ethnicity, Insurgency, and Civil War," *American Political Science Review*, Vol. 97, No. 1, February 2003, pp. 75–90; Michael W. Doyle and Nicholas Sambanis, *Making War and Building Peace*, Princeton, N.J.: Princeton University Press, 2006.

6   U.S. Army and U.S. Marine Corps, *Counterinsurgency Field Manual*, Chicago: University of Chicago Press, 2007, p. 179.

is more likely through the implementation of "*national* programs that enable a government to perform a state function through its territory."[7]

Top-down strategies reflect the conventional wisdom among many policymakers and academics.[8] As one study concludes, creating sustainable peace requires building strong central government institutions that can provide effective administration over the country.[9] According to this argument, national governance is critical. *Governance*, as used here, is defined as the set of institutions by which authority in a country is exercised.[10] It includes the ability to establish law and order, effectively manage resources, and implement sound policies from a central government.

However, the top-down model faces several challenges. First, the strength of state institutions varies widely for cultural, economic, social, and other reasons.[11] Many Western countries are characterized by strong central government institutions, with power coming from the top down. But other countries—including many across South Asia and Africa—have rich tribal and local cultures, in which power frequently emerges from the bottom up.[12] This is also true of security forces, which can have a range of centralized and decentralized

---

[7] Ashraf Ghani and Clare Lockhart, *Fixing Failed States: A Framework for Rebuilding a Fractured World*, New York: Oxford University Press, 2008, p. 14. Emphasis added.

[8] Among academic works see, for example, Francis Fukuyama, *State-Building: Governance and World Order in the 21st Century*, Ithaca, N.Y.: Cornell University Press, 2004; Simon Chesterman, *You, the People: The United Nations, Transitional Administration, and State-building*, New York: Oxford University Press, 2004; Stephen D. Krasner, "Sharing Sovereignty: New Institutions for Collapsed and Failing States," *International Security*, Vol. 29, No. 2, Autumn 2004; Roland Paris, *At War's End: Building Peace After Civil Conflict*, New York: Cambridge University Press, 2004.

[9] Paris, *At War's End*.

[10] World Bank, *Governance Matters, 2006: Worldwide Governance Indicators*, Washington, D.C.: World Bank, 2006, p. 2.

[11] See, for example, Stephen D. Krasner, *Sovereignty: Organized Hypocrisy*, Princeton, N.J.: Princeton University Press, 1999.

[12] On decentralized systems in Africa, see, for example, Meyer Fortes and Edward Evans-Pritchard, *African Political Systems*, New York: Oxford University Press, 1970.

arrangements.[13] Recent anthropological studies, for instance, conclude that Afghanistan continues to be decentralized. "One does not seek justice through government institutions (which often do not exist)," writes Thomas Barfield, "but by mobilizing the kin group to seek retribution or compensations."[14]

Second, as Francis Fukuyama argues, outsiders have a limited ability to shape local societies and improve institutional capacity. Most outsiders fail to realize that there is no optimal form of state organization and that there are not always clear-cut "best practices" to solve public administration problems. Rather, state-building is context specific. States are not black boxes, as economic theories long assumed. Instead, history, culture, and social structures influence the preferences and utility functions of individuals. Some areas, such as central banking, are more susceptible to technocratic reform by outsiders. Other areas, such as education or law, are more difficult to reform because performance is harder to measure and because transaction volumes are higher. The challenge, then, is to combine a general knowledge of administrative practices with a deep understanding of local conditions.[15] In most countries, this requires a combination of top-down and bottom-up efforts.

According to NATO's own assessments, the challenges in Afghanistan's security sector are acute. General McChrystal's 2009 assessment bluntly noted that "we face not only a resilient and growing insurgency; there is also a crisis of confidence among Afghans—in both their government and the international community—that undermines our credibility and emboldens the insurgents."[16]

---

[13] See, for example, David Bayley, *Patterns of Policing*, New Brunswick, N.J.: Rutgers University Press, 1985, pp. 53–73.

[14] Thomas J. Barfield, "Weapons of the Not So Weak in Afghanistan: Pashtun Agrarian Structure and Tribal Organization for Times of War and Peace," paper presented to the Agrarian Studies Colloquium Series, Yale University, February 23, 2007.

[15] Fukuyama, *State-Building*.

[16] McChrystal, "COMISAF's Initial Assessment," p. 1-1.

Security of the Afghan Population

Polling data provide one metric for gauging local perceptions of security. In Afghanistan, public opinion data indicate that insecurity remains one of the country's biggest problems. This information is important because it reflects the views of local Afghans, the center of gravity in any counterinsurgency. For instance, data released in early 2010 reported that nearly 50 percent of Afghans thought that their security from crime and violence was "somewhat" or "very" bad.[17] Another set of data from 2008 indicated that nearly 50 percent of Afghans "often" or "sometimes" feared for their personal safety or that of their family. Nearly two-thirds (61 percent) said they had "some fear" or "a lot of fear" when traveling from one part of Afghanistan to another.[18] Incidents of kidnapping appear to have increased over the past several years as the Taliban, other militant groups, and criminal syndicates have set up checkpoints along roads.[19]

Figure 2.1 highlights Afghan perceptions of security by province. It divides areas of insecurity into four categories. They range from areas in which 75 to 100 percent of respondents acknowledged they "often" or "sometimes" feared for their personal safety or for that of their family, to areas in which only 0 to 25 percent of respondents feared for their safety. The most insecure provinces of the country are Helmand and Wardak, followed by a swath of provinces in the west (Herat, Farah, Ghor, Badghis), north (Sar-e Pul), south (Zabul and Kandahar), and east (Khost, Ghazni, Logar, Paktia, Kabul, Laghman, and Nuristan).[20]

This geographic breakdown highlights several themes. First, significant levels of insecurity have engulfed more than one-half the country. Afghan concerns about personal safety were most significant

---

[17] ABC, BBC, and ARD, "Afghanistan: Where Things Stand," poll, January 2010.

[18] Asia Foundation, *Afghanistan in 2008: A Survey of the Afghan People*, Kabul, 2008. Also see Asia Foundation, *Afghanistan in 2009: A Survey of the Afghan People*, Kabul, 2009.

[19] Amnesty International, "Amnesty International Contacts Taliban Spokesperson, Urges Release of Hostages," New York, August 2, 2007.

[20] Asia Foundation, *Afghanistan in 2008*.

Figure 2.1
Areas of Insecurity

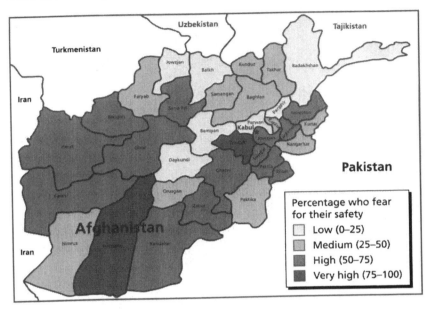

SOURCE: Asia Foundation, *Afghanistan in 2008.*
RAND MG1002-2.1

along an arc that begins in the west, creeps southward through such provinces as Helmand and Kandahar, continues northeast along the Afghanistan-Pakistan border through Paktia and Khowst, and then moves into such provinces as Wardak and Kabul. When asked to rate their ability to move safely in their area and district, the percentage of those who said "quite bad" or "very bad" was highest in this arc: 54 percent in Herat, 70 percent in Helmand, 65 percent in Kandahar, and 63 percent in Ghazni. Second, the threats that concern Afghans varied widely across the country. When asked what kind of violence or crime respondents or someone in their family experienced in the past year, concerns about the insurgency are highest in the south and east, as are concerns regarding kidnapping, suicide attacks, and the actions of foreign forces. But Afghans face high levels of physical attack and beating in most areas of the country, from Wardak (79 percent) to

Khowst (56 percent) and Jowzjan (50 percent). Racketeering and burglary also extend throughout most of the country.[21]

Although there are disagreements about the force ratios needed to protect a local population, we judge that there is a gap in force requirements to protect the Afghan population. Some studies argue that a rough estimate needed to win a counterinsurgency is 20 security personnel per 1,000 inhabitants.[22] As the U.S. Army and Marine Corps counterinsurgency manual notes: "Twenty counterinsurgents per 1,000 residents is often considered the minimum troop density required for effective COIN operations; however as with any fixed ratio, such calculations remain very dependent upon the situation."[23] This translates into a force requirement of approximately 660,000 personnel for a population of approximately 33 million people. But this still leaves several critical questions unanswered. What percentage of these forces should be international, and what percentage should be Afghan? Among Afghan forces, what percentage should be national, and what percentage should be local forces? Even among Afghan local forces, what type should they be? There are, after all, multiple options, from the Afghan Public Protection Program in Wardak to more traditional lashkars and arbakai.

There is no clear-cut answer—and certainly no magic number—of U.S. and Afghan forces. However, local perceptions about the United States have deteriorated over the past several years from their

---

[21] Asia Foundation, *Afghanistan in 2008*.

[22] James T. Quinlivan, "Force Requirements in Security Operations," *Parameters*, Vol. 25, No. 4, Winter 1995–1996; James Dobbins, John G. McGinn, Keith Crane, Seth G. Jones, Rollie Lal, Andrew Rathmell, Rachel M. Swanger, and Anga R. Timilsina, *America's Role in Nation-Building: From Germany to Iraq*, Santa Monica, Calif.: RAND Corporation, MR-1753-RC, 2003; James Dobbins, Seth G. Jones, Keith Crane, Andrew Rathmell, Brett Steele, Richard Teltschik, and Anga R. Timilsina, *The UN's Role in Nation-Building: From the Congo to Iraq*, Santa Monica, Calif.: RAND Corporation, MG-304-RC, 2005.

[23] U.S. Army and U.S. Marine Corps, *Counterinsurgency*, FM 3-24, MCWP 3-33.5, Washington, D.C.: Headquarters Department of the Army and Headquarters Marine Corps Combat Development Command, December 2006, p. 1-13.

high in 2001.[24] This suggests that the percentage of Afghan security forces (both national and local) should increase in the south and east to help counter the perception that U.S. and NATO forces are becoming a foreign army of occupation, which bolsters Taliban propaganda. Current NATO operational guidelines stress avoiding civilian casualties, searching homes, breaking down doors, and any other practices that have alienated Pashtuns. However, this population-centric counterinsurgency approach must be understood in the context of the publicly stated 2011 downsizing the U.S. president has announced, as well as declining political support from NATO countries, such as Canada, the Netherlands, and the United Kingdom. Given this context, turning the war over to Afghans should be a pressing and time-sensitive goal.

Given the increasing Afghan aversion to outside forces, we judge that it is unlikely that the United States and NATO will defeat the Taliban and other insurgent groups in Afghanistan through a heavy international military footprint that tries to clear territory, hold it, and build reconstruction and development projects. Virtually all counterinsurgency studies—from David Galula to Roger Trinquier—have focused on building the capacity of local forces.[25] Victory is usually a function of the struggle between the local government and insurgents. Most outside forces are unlikely to remain for the duration of any counterinsurgency, at least as a major combatant force.[26] Most domestic populations tire of engaging their forces in struggles overseas, as even the Soviet population did in Afghanistan in the 1980s. In addition, a population may interpret a large foreign presence as an

---

[24] See, for example, ABC, BBC, and ARD, "Afghanistan: Where Things Stand," poll, January 2010; ABC, BBC, and ARD, "Afghanistan: Where Things Stand," poll, 2009.

[25] Galula, *Counterinsurgency Warfare*; Roger Trinquier, *Modern Warfare: A French View of Counterinsurgency*, trans. Daniel Lee, New York: Praeger, 2006.

[26] Kimberly Marten Zisk, *Enforcing the Peace: Learning from the Imperial Past*, New York: Columbia University Press, 2004; Amitai Etzioni, "A Self-Restrained Approach to Nation-Building by Foreign Powers," *International Affairs*, Vol. 80, No. 1, 2004; Amitai Etzioni, *From Empire to Community: A New Approach to International Relations*, New York: Palgrave Macmillan, 2004; Stephen T. Hosmer, *The Army's Role in Counterinsurgency and Insurgency*, Santa Monica, Calif: RAND Corporation, R-3947-A, 1990, pp. 30–31.

occupation, eliciting nationalist reactions that impede success.[27] If, instead, indigenous people take the lead, it can provide a focus for national aspirations and show the population that they—and not foreign forces—control their destiny.

Conclusions

Current efforts to establish security from the top down and *only* through Afghan national institutions have failed for several reasons. First, there are not enough—nor will there likely be enough—national forces to protect the local population, especially in rural areas of the country. Second, Afghan national forces, especially ANP, remain incompetent, ill-prepared, and unpopular. NATO's own assessments have concluded that, "Due to a lack of overall strategic coherence and insufficient resources, the ANP has not been organized, trained, and equipped to operate effectively as a counter-insurgency force."[28] Third, many Afghans in rural areas—especially in Pashtun areas—have historically eschewed central government forces providing permanent security in their villages. Power in Pashtun areas tends to be local. This is certainly true today, making it critical to understand local institutions that can provide village-level security.

---

[27] David M. Edelstein, "Occupational Hazards: Why Military Occupations Succeed or Fail," *International Security*, Vol. 29, No. 1, Summer 2004, p. 51.

[28] McChrystal, "COMISAF's Initial Assessment," p. G-2.

CHAPTER THREE

Local Dynamics and Community Policing

While some have argued that the insurgency cuts across multiple ethnic groups in Afghanistan, it is primarily being waged in rural Pashtun areas.[1] The Taliban and other groups have co-opted and coerced some Tajiks, Uzbeks, Hazaras, and others. But it is not a coincidence that all the major insurgent groups are Pashtun, from Mullah Mohammad Omar's Taliban to the Haqqani network and Gulbuddin Hekmatyar's Hezb-i-Islami. This reality makes it important to understand the social, cultural, political, and economic structures in Pashtun society. This chapter begins by examining the local nature of power in Afghanistan (especially in Pashtun areas), then outlines the traditional practice of community policing.

Debating the Role of Tribes

For some, tribes have largely ceased to exist or been irrevocably weakened. In *Anthropology Today*, Roberto Gonzalez notes that the term *tribe* is vague and that profound disagreement exists among anthropologists over how to define a tribe and tribal culture. "Recent interest in Afghanistan's 'tribes' appears to stem from an increasingly desperate political situation," he argues. "Few anthropologists today would consider using the term 'tribe' as an analytical category, or even as a

---

[1] See, for example, Sippi Azerbaijani Moghaddam, "Northern Exposure for the Taliban," in Antonio Giustozzi, ed., *Decoding the New Taliban: Insights from the Afghan Field*, New York: Columbia University Press, 2009.

concept for practical application."[2] A U.S. army assessment concluded that "a singular focus on 'tribe' as the central organizational principle of Afghan society implies a need to identify leaders, institutions, and relationships that may not exist."[3] This argument assumes that too much emphasis has been placed on tribes and tribal engagement in Afghanistan.[4] Instead, tribal identity is described as one of many forms of identification among Pashtuns.

What is missing in these arguments is an appreciation of the interplay between identity, structure, and culture. Pashtuns are organized according to a patrilineal segmentary lineage system. This presupposes that the tribe will segment, or split, among multiple kin groups that will engage in competition with each other most of the time. When a common enemy outside the tribe poses an existential threat, the different segments tend to band together—since they are related by common descent—until the emergency is over. Traditional rivalry among patrilineal cousins is so pronounced among the Pashtuns, partly because they compete for the same inheritance, that it has given rise to a term, *tarburwali* (law of the cousins).

The Yousufzai Pashtun *khan khel* system demonstrates the melding of kinship and locality, along with social relationships, to produce a social grouping that is a primary locus of identity, politics, and military action. The *khel*, which can be used to denote tribe, subtribe, or clan—or to serve as a suffix for geographic place names—is theoretically based on common descent. However, *khels* are integrally related to a *khan*, an overall chief, whom community members follow. The key aspect of the *khan khel* system, for our purposes, is that the followers of the *khan* are not only fellow Yousufzai but may also include

---

2   Alberto Gonzalez, "Going Tribal: Notes on Pacification in the 21st Century," *Anthropology Today*, Vol. 25, No. 2, April 2009; see also Antonio Giustozzi and Noor Ullah, *Tribes and Warlords in Southern Afghanistan, 1980–2005*, London: Crisis States Research Centre, Working Paper No. 7, September 2006, pp. 1–22.

3   U.S. Army Training and Doctrine Command, G2 Human Terrain System, *My Cousin's Enemy Is My Friend: A Study of Pashtun "Tribes,"* Fort Leavenworth, Kan.: United States Army, September 2009, p. 24.

4   On tribal engagement, see, for example, Jim Gant, *One Tribe at a Time*, Los Angeles: Nine Sisters Imports, 2009.

non-Pashtuns, such as Gujar herdsmen who are attached to the *khan*'s lands or household, as well as families of various castes who are similarly attached. These may be Pashtuns or Kohistanis—or even Hindus or other non-Muslims. All are considered part of the *khan khel*, occupying widely divergent status, rights, and duties. During the days of endemic tribal warfare, *khan khels* would fight as a group for their *khan* much like medieval peasants fought for their feudal lords. Indeed, *khan khels* often continued as a distinct entity long after the original *khan* died and was replaced by his sons and grandsons. A *qawm* works in a similar fashion, without the central role of the dominant *khan* family. Both are aspects of the traditional tribal system in which localism is a key facet of tribalism.

According to this view of tribal structure, competing identities of tribe, subtribe, clan, *qawm*, or locality are all within the overarching tribal system. A *qawm* is a unit of identification and solidarity that could be based on kinship, residence, or occupation.[5] It is a flexible term that can be used to describe a large tribe or a small, isolated village and is used to differentiate "us" versus "them." Saying that Pashtuns in a particular area identify only with the particular valley in which they live, as opposed to a tribe, suggests a misunderstanding of how a decentralized tribal system works. Tribalism is localism. There are many examples of segmented tribes that are deeply divided. But this does not make them any less "tribal." Moreover, it would be a mistake to dismiss the overarching tribal identity—such as a Durrani or Ghilzai—because it remains important for some Pashtuns.

There are also a variety of ethnic groups in Afghanistan. Both a tribe and an ethnic group may claim a common ancestry, history, language, and culture. However, ethnic groups—often formed by a past amalgamation of tribes—lack a tribal structure. For instance, ethnic groups usually do not have councils of elders making decisions for the group. Most importantly, the self-identity of an ethnic group is much larger in scope, although ethnic groups have clans and extended families. Rather than the local orientation typical of tribal people, ethnic

---

[5] David Phillips, *Afghanistan: A History of Utilization of Tribal Auxiliaries*, Williamsburg, Va.: Tribal Analysis Center, 2008, p. 1.

groups can aspire to create their own nation-states. This crystallizes the difference with a tribe, a nonstate form of social organization. Especially when religious affiliation and ethnic identity become fused, the struggle to form ethnically based states has led to tremendous bloodshed, as in the breakup of Yugoslavia among Croat, Serb, and Bosniak ethnicities.

By these criteria, Afghanistan's Tajiks, Uzbeks, Hazaras, and Turkmen should be considered ethnic groups, not tribes.[6] Indeed, there are nation-states associated with the Tajiks (Tajikistan), the Uzbeks (Uzbekistan), and the Turkmen (Turkmenistan). Pashtuns present an analytic challenge because they can be considered both as an ethnic group and a confederation of tribes. A strong case can be made for Pashtun ethnic nationalism, bolstered by long-standing agitation for the creation of an independent "Pashtunistan." Yet the Pashtuns also exhibit characteristics of tribal people. Tribes exist in Pashtun areas, which include parts of western, southern, eastern, and small sections of northern Afghanistan. There are also non-Pashtun tribes, such as the Nuristanis in northeastern Afghanistan.[7]

Local Dynamics

Despite these realities, tribal structures have eroded over the last century for a variety of reasons.[8] Amir Abdur Rahman, for example, who reigned from 1880 to 1901, uprooted many tribal communities with the overriding goal of strengthening the central government and delib-

---

6   Thomas J. Barfield, "Culture and Custom in Nation-Building: Law in Afghanistan," *Maine Law Review*, Vol. 60, No. 2, Summer 2008, p. 354.

7   See, for example, M. Nazif Shahrani, "Introduction: Marxist 'Revolution' and Islamic Resistance in Afghanistan," in M. Nazif Shahrani and Robert L. Canfield, eds., *Revolutions and Rebellions in Afghanistan: Anthropological Perspectives*, Berkeley, Calif.: Institute of International Studies, University of California, Berkeley, 1984.

8   Some of the best anthropological works on Afghanistan include Louis Dupree, *Afghanistan*, New York: Oxford University Press, 1997; Richard Tapper, ed., *The Conflict of Tribe and State in Iran and Afghanistan*, New York: St. Martin's Press, 1983; Shahrani and Canfield, eds., *Revolutions and Rebellions*; Fredrik Barth, ed., *Ethnic Groups and Boundaries: The Social Organization of Culture Difference*, Boston: Little, Brown, 1969.

erately weakening the tribal system. Even though he was a Pashtun himself, the "Iron Emir" resettled various Pashtun tribes and subtribes as punishment for rebellion or to use them as counterweights against hostile non-Pashtun tribes or ethnic groups. He declared jihad against Hazaras and conducted a campaign of ethnic cleansing, which left pockets of Pashtun settlers in the north, where they remain today.[9] The 1978 rebellion against the communist regime initiated a cycle of warfare causing massive displacement among Afghan tribes. During the ten-year war against the Soviet occupation, millions of refugees fled to Pakistan, and there was extensive internal migration within Afghanistan. Rather than restore peace, the departure of the Soviets in 1989 ushered in another civil war among competing Afghan factions that triggered mass migration. Since then, the tribal structure has evolved because of war, droughts, migration patterns, sedentarization, and other factors. Sedentarization is the process in which tribes cease seasonal or nomadic lifestyles and settle down in permanent habitats.[10]

Social instability is pronounced in such areas as the Helmand River valley, where the U.S. government funded major infrastructure irrigation projects beginning in the 1950s, including the Kajaki dam in northern Helmand.[11] The Afghan government brought masses of settlers from outside the region, upsetting the previous demographic balance. According to the work of Nick Cullather, "not only did [the Kajaki dam project] entail the forced displacement and resettlement of local populations, which caused serious conflicts, but it proved detrimental to the local economy, and also raised the salinity level of the soil."[12] Natives and settlers alike fled en masse during the Soviet

---

[9] Thomas J. Barfield, "Problems in Establishing Legitimacy in Afghanistan," *Iranian Studies*, Vol. 37, No. 2, June 2004.

[10] Barnett R. Rubin, *The Fragmentation of Afghanistan: State Formation and Collapse in the International System*, 2nd ed., New Haven, Conn.: Yale University Press, 2002; Roohullah Ramin, "Afghanistan: Exploring the Dynamics of Sociopolitical Strife and Persistence of the Insurgency," Ottawa: Pearson Peacekeeping Centre, Occasional Paper 2, 2008, pp. 1–38.

[11] Dupree, *Afghanistan*, pp. 499–507.

[12] Nick Cullather, "Damming Afghanistan: Modernization in a Buffer State," *The Journal of American History*, Vol. 89, No. 2, September 2002, pp. 25–30; Feliz Kuntzsch, *Afghanistan's*

occupation and the subsequent civil wars. It is difficult to generalize about the tribal structure today, since the structure and inclinations of a tribe or subtribe in one area may be very different from those of the same tribe or subtribe in another area. Other identity markers can also transcend tribal structures, such as reputations earned during the anti-Soviet jihad, land ownership, or money earned through licit or illicit activities (such as the drug trade or road taxes). In some areas, Taliban leaders have also elevated the role of mullahs and other religious leaders to assist in the function of sharia (Islamic law) courts.

Despite these developments, however, power remains local in Pashtun areas.[13] Public opinion polls strongly indicate that Afghans turn to community leaders—especially jirga or shura elders—to solve their problems.[14] Pashtuns have long based identity on a nested set of clans and lineages that stem from a common ancestor. In the absence of strong government institutions, descent groups help Pashtuns organize economic production, preserve political order, and defend the group from outside threats.[15] Afghan tribal organizations use common descent through the male line to define membership, but these bonds tend to be weaker in urban areas, where central government control is stronger. "If all politics is local, then Afghan politics is local and personal as well," notes anthropologist Thomas Barfield. "The social structure of communities is based either on the tribe (where kinship relations determine social organization and basic political alliances) or the locality (where people identify themselves in terms of common place)."[16]

Rocky Road to Modernity, Québec: Université Laval, Institut Québécois des Hautes Études Internationales, July 2008.

[13] See, for example, Tribal Liaison Office, *Good Governance in Tribal Areas Kandahar Research Project: Research Report*, Kabul, 2005; Thomas H. Johnson and M. Chris Mason, "No Sign Until the Burst of Fire: Understanding the Pakistan-Afghanistan Frontier," *International Security*, Vol. 32, No. 4, Spring 2008.

[14] See, for example, Asia Foundation, *Afghanistan in 2009*, p. 197.

[15] Barfield, "Weapons of the Not So Weak in Afghanistan."

[16] Barfield, "Culture and Custom," p. 353.

The Role of *Pashtunwali*

Pashtunwali (law of the Pashtuns) shapes daily life through such concepts as *badal* (revenge), *melmastia* (hospitality), *ghayrat* (honor), and *nanawati* (sanctuary). *Pashtunwali* is an oral tradition that consists of general principles and practices (*tsal*) applied to specific cases. Jirgas and shuras are instrumental in enforcing *Pashtunwali* through their decisionmaking at the local level. Historically, a *jirga* is a temporary council established to address specific issues, while a *shura* is a more-permanent consultative council. In practice, however, the two terms are often used interchangeably.[17]

Pashtunwali is a form of customary law, which can be defined as the way in which local communities resolve disputes in the absence of state authority—or sometimes in opposition to it. According to one tradition, conflict generally arises because of *zar* (gold), *zan* (women), or *zamin* (land). Unlike formal criminal codes, in which guilty individuals pay fines to the government or are imprisoned, Pashtun customary law seeks compensation based on social reconciliation. Community members are the primary fact finders and decisionmakers, although respected outsiders may be used as well. The local jirga fulfills the key functions of arbitration and judgment. These jirgas, for example, can demand that the wrongdoer apologize publicly to the victim and make a payment for *sharm* (shame).[18]

As in other examples of tribal legal systems in the Middle East and North Africa, mutually accepted compensation is a key aspect to the victim and the family. This covers a wide variety of crimes up to homicide, which would require a substantial "blood payment" to avoid the "eye for an eye" vengeance sanctioned by *Pashtunwali*. In this type of tribal law, the perpetrator of the offense and the victim are viewed collectively. Indeed, the perpetrator's family shares culpability, and the victim's family is also considered victimized (and therefore often shares

---

[17] See, for example, Tribal Liaison Office, *Good Governance in Tribal Areas*.

[18] Barfield, "Culture and Custom." Also see, for example, Fredrik Barth, "Pathan Identity and Its Maintenance," in Barth, ed., *Ethnic Groups and Boundaries*, 1969.

in the compensation). This collective view of culpability has fueled blood feuds for centuries.

Tribes tend to be more hierarchical in southern and western Afghanistan than in eastern Afghanistan. Two tribal confederations, the Durrani and Ghilzai, subsume more than two-thirds of all Afghan Pashtuns. Figure 3.1 breaks down the relationships among southern Durrani tribes. In accordance with the segmentary lineage system, these tribes are further subdivided along clan and other lines. Intense fighting is common among subtribes, such as between the Hassanzai, Khalozai, and Pirzai subtribes of the Alizai in Helmand Province. Figure 3.2 highlights the key Ghilzai tribes, many of which dwell in highland areas of the east. Some argue that these tribes are much stronger than in lowland areas.[19]

In addition to the Durranis and Ghilzai, Pashtun tribes include the Wardak, Jaji, Tani, Zadran, Mangal, Safi, Mohmand, and Shinwari. Our analysis indicates that tribal and other local affiliations tend to be more pronounced in rural areas. In some urban areas, such as the cities of Kandahar and Kabul, tribal and other local ties appear to have weakened for many Pashtuns.

One testament to the importance of tribes and other local institutions is the Taliban's strategy of co-opting or coercing them. The Taliban has traditionally represented a rise to power of mullahs, and senior Taliban leaders adhere to a radical interpretation of Deobandi Islam.[20] Deobandism is a school of thought that originated at the Dar ul-Ulum madrassa (Islamic school) in 1867 in Deoband, India, just north of Delhi. But a closer look at the Taliban's strategy in rural Pashtun areas indicates a strong proclivity toward negotiating with tribal and other local leaders. In addition, a variety of social, cultural, and religious factors have driven some Pashtuns to join or support the Taliban, especially if it helps a young man enhance the prestige of his family among both *azzizan* (near and distant relatives) and *dokhmanon* (ene-

---

19 Thomas Ruttig, "Loya Paktia's Insurgency: The Haqqani Network as an Autonomous Entity," in Giustozzi, ed., *Decoding the New Taliban*, 2009.

20 See, for example, Thomas H. Johnson and M. Chris Mason, "Understanding the Taliban Insurgency in Afghanistan," *Orbis*, Vol. 51, No. 1, Winter 2007.

Figure 3.1
Durrani Tribes

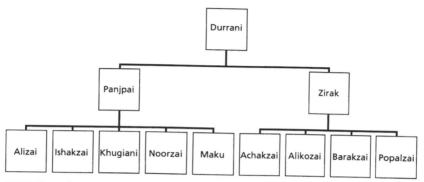

SOURCE: Author interviews.
RAND MG1002-3.1

Figure 3.2
Ghilzai Tribes

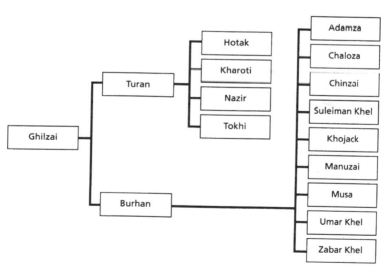

SOURCE: Author interviews.
RAND MG1002-3.2

mies). In broad terms, the Taliban aim to co-opt or coerce local leaders and their support bases by taking advantage of grievances against the government or international forces, conducting targeted assassinations against those who collaborate or work with the Afghan government or international forces, and capitalizing on Taliban momentum (and the perception of a "domino effect") to increase their appeal to locals. In April 2009, the Taliban announced the beginning of Operation *Nasrat* (Victory), noting that they would continue to use "ambushes, offensives, explosions, martyrdom-seeking attacks and surprise attacks."[21]

Taliban commanders tend to use their knowledge of Pashtun tribes, subtribes, clans, and *qawms* to approach local leaders and convince them that resistance is futile, prompting them to either disband or join the Taliban. The Taliban often appoints commanders who come from local subtribes or clans to more effectively reach out to the population. These commanders have often effectively reached out to tribes that have been marginalized by tribes favored by the government.[22]

For example, Ishakzais control the Taliban strongholds in the Washir mountains in Helmand, and many Taliban commanders from the strategic area of Marjeh are also Ishakzais. According to some reports, the Ishakzai joined the Taliban partly in reaction to the policies of Governor Sher Muhammad Akhunzada, who deliberately deprived them of resources to favor his own Hassanzai Alizai tribesmen. In 2006, the Taliban successfully took over parts of Sangin District in Helmand Province by supporting the marginalized Ishakzai tribes. In using its patronage to support a favored few tribes and tribal leaders, especially in the south, the Afghan government has potentially created or worsened many of the tribal rivalries the Taliban exploits. President Karzai has tended to favor such individuals as Sher Muhammad Akhunzada (Alizai), Jan Mohammad Khan (Popalzai), Ahmad Wali Karzai (Popalzai), and Kalimullah Nequib (Alikozai).

---

21 Taliban Voice of Jihad Online, April 29, 2009.

22 See, for example, Johnson and Mason, "Understanding the Taliban Insurgency in Afghanistan"; Tribal Analysis Center, "The Panjpai Relationship with the Other Durranis," research paper, Williamsburg, Va., January 2009; Tribal Analysis Center, "The Quetta Shura: A Tribal Analysis," research paper, Williamsburg, Va., October 2009.

Many of the tribal feuds in Helmand have resulted from power struggles involving drug trafficking, land, and influence. In 2009, local Alikozai and Ishakzai leaders fought over narcotics in Sangin, and Ishakzai, Noorzai, and other tribal leaders fought over control of Marjeh. In addition, the relationships between the Taliban, local powerbrokers, and narcotics elements facilitate Taliban efforts to consolidate their presence and influence through the province.[23] The Taliban has effectively exploited many of these fissures, while Afghan and NATO governments have not systematically engaged at this level.

In addition to Helmand, the insurgency in Oruzgan has been a "continuation of what has become a very violent way of waging local power struggles" among tribes, subtribes, and other local actors.[24] In such western provinces as Herat and Farah, the Taliban has relied on local Pashtun networks to expand its power base, including among Noorzai communities.[25] Other insurgents have also developed bottom-up strategies and reached out to tribes and other local communities. One of the Haqqani network's strongest support bases is the Mezi subtribe of the Zadran tribe, located in Paktia, Paktika, and Khowst provinces. The Haqqani network has also co-opted a range of *kuchis*, nomadic tribes, in Paktia and Khowst, and developed a close relationship with Mullah Nazir's group across the border in Pakistan, which has a significant support base among the Kaka Khel subtribe of the Ahmadzai Waziris. In addition, the Mansur network in eastern Afghanistan developed a support base among the Sahak subtribe of the Andar Pashtuns.[26]

---

[23] Gretchen Peters, *Seeds of Terror: How Heroin Is Bankrolling the Taliban and al Qaeda*, New York: St. Martin's Press, 2009; Thomas H. Johnson, "Financing Afghan Terrorism: Thugs, Drugs, and Creative Movements of Money," in Jeanne K. Giraldo and Harold A. Trinkunas, eds., *Terrorism Financing and State Responses: A Comparative Perspective*, Stanford, Calif.: Stanford University Press, 2007.

[24] Martine van Bijlert, "Unruly Commanders and Violent Power Struggles: Taliban Networks in Uruzgan," in Giustozzi, ed., *Decoding the New Taliban*, pp. 155–178.

[25] Antonio Giustozzi, "The Taliban's Marches: Herat, Farah, Baghdis and Ghor," in Giustozzi, ed., *Decoding the New Taliban*, 2009, pp. 211–230.

[26] Ruttig, "Loya Paktia's Insurgency."

Local Policing

Tribes and other local communities throughout the world tend to have some form of raising armed groups from within their ranks.[27] In situations of endemic tribal warfare, a dependable mechanism for raising an armed force is critical for survival. These armed groups often are organized along kinship lines but can also be based on residence. Local councils usually put out the call to arms, but shamans and other religious leaders, or influential chiefs, can also do so. Among the Pashtuns of Afghanistan and Pakistan, there are at least five institutions for organizing local forces. In each case, they implement the decisions of local jirgas or shuras.[28] These forces are significantly different from warlord militias. Warlords are charismatic leaders with autonomous control of security forces who are able to monopolize violence within a given territory.[29] Their militias are beholden to individuals, not to a community, making them fundamentally different from community policing forces. Warlords view themselves as above the tribe and, unlike traditional forces, do not answer to the jirgas or shuras.

Different villages may use different terms to describe similar community forces.[30] Although names and characteristics may vary regionally, we have encountered at least five major institutions:

- *Tsalweshtai*—This generally refers to a guard force of approximately 40 men drawn from various subsections of the tribe. A tsalweshtai is appointed for a special purpose, such as protecting a valley from raiding groups. There is a specific tribal injunction

---

[27] Alan Warren, "'Bullocks Treading Down Wasps'? The British Indian Army in Waziristan in the 1930s," *South Asia*, Vol. 19, No. 2, 1996.

[28] Phillips, *Afghanistan*, p. 1.

[29] Antonio Giustozzi, *Empires of Mud: Wars and Warlords in Afghanistan*, New York: Columbia University Press, 2009, p. 5. Also see, for example, Kimberly Marten, "Warlordism in Comparative Perspective," *International Security*, Vol. 31, No. 3, Winter 2006–2007.

[30] Mohammed Osman Tariq, *Tribal Security System (Arbakai) in Southeast Afghanistan*, London: Crisis States Research Centre, December 2008, pp. 1–19; Shahmahmood Miakhel, "The Importance of Tribal Structures and Pakhtunwali in Afghanistan: Their Role in Security and Governance," in Arpita Basu Roy, ed., *Challenges and Dilemmas of State-Building in Afghanistan: Report of a Study Trip to Kabul*, Delhi: Shipra Publications, 2008.

to ensure that no blood feud results if a tsalweshtai kills someone while on duty. This type of force may be more common in the northwestern portion of Pashtun territory in Afghanistan.

- *Arbakai*—Essentially a community police force, this group implements the local jirga's decisions and has immunity from these decisions.[31] The term arbakai has generally been used for community police in such provinces as Paktia, Khowst, and Paktika, although we have encountered local leaders in southern Afghanistan that use the term as well. Locals in some areas of the east, including around Shkin, Paktika, use other terms—such as chalweshtai—instead of arbakai to describe the same type of force.

- *Chagha*—A chagha is a group of fighters raised spontaneously within a specific village facing a bandit raid, robbery, livestock rustling, or similar offense. Chagha is also the word for the drum that is used to inform the people of the need to organize and to drive off invaders.

- *Chalweshtai*—This force is larger than a tsalweshtai. Young men from each family volunteer to implement jirga or shura decisions that may involve warfare, jihad, or even self-help projects. As with the arbakai, the actions of the chalweshtai are sanctioned by the community elders. While a chalweshtai may engage in community projects, such as digging a canal or building a dam, the more common employment is in crime prevention on roads they are assigned to police.

- *Lashkar*—This force serves a particular *qawm* and is often used for offensive purposes. A lashkar can be small, such as a dozen men attacking a nearby village during a family feud, or very large, such as the 50,000-man force Pakistan sent into Kashmir in 1947 and 1948. The western equivalent is North America's Native Ameri-

---

[31] Susanne Schmeidl and Masood Karokhail, "The Role of Non-State Actors in 'Community-Based Policing': An Exploration of the Arbakai (Tribal Police) in South-Eastern Afghanistan," *Contemporary Security Policy*, Vol. 30, No. 2, August 2009.

can "war party." Lashkars can be used in jihad or can be used to oppose a policy of a government.[32]

Locals elsewhere also use other terms—for instance, *mahali satoonkay* or *milli mahali satunki* (local protectors or local defenders) in such areas as Arghandab, Kandahar—to describe similar, village-level forces.[33] Today, the call to arms for any of these groups may more likely be communicated by cell phone or loudspeakers mounted on a village mosque.

Lashkars tend to be different from the other institutions, partly because they are usually offensive, intended to attack a specific target and then disband. Lashkars can sometimes fight effectively and have a long record of activity in the Afghanistan-Pakistan border region. In their biographies, the walis of Swat frequently mention their use of lashkars to crush enemies and maintain power. They ensured that their lashkars had enough food, weapons, and good leadership to achieve their objectives.[34] Yet lashkars are often insufficient to confront a well-organized, well-armed, and ruthless insurgency. Perhaps more importantly, lashkars can sometimes get unwieldy and can be manipulated by individual commanders, who use them to gain—and maintain—power.

In contrast, arbakai are generally defensive and tend to be small. As one study concluded, "their jurisdiction is limited to the territory governed by the respective jirga/shura they are mandated by" and "if a village raises an arbakai it cannot work anywhere else (this creates parallels to neighborhood watch committees)."[35] Arbakai and other local institutions, such as chalweshtai, have often been unpaid and carry responsibilities that the tribe or community approves of as a public good. Serving as an arbakai member is considered an honor, while

---

[32] Phillips, *Afghanistan*, pp. 1–2.

[33] Author interview with tribal leaders in Kandahar, December 2009.

[34] Miangul Jahanzeb and Frederick Barth, *The Last Wali of Swat: An Autobiography*, Bangkok: Orchid Press, 2006; Syed Miangul Faroosh, *The Wali of Swat*, Peshawar: Mian Gul Shahzada Mohammed Abdul Haq Jehanzeb, 1983.

[35] Schmeidl and Karokhail, "The Role of Non-State Actors," p. 324.

belonging to a militia is often considered shameful.[36] While each arbakai has a clear leader, they are accountable to the council (jirga or shura) that created the arbakai, as well as to the community. In sum, their loyalty is to their communities, not to an individual leader.[37] The responsibility of any specific arbakai differs from one tribe to another, although they do have common tasks and duties:

- Implement the jirga's decisions.
- Maintain law and order.
- Protect and defend borders and boundaries of the tribe or community.[38]

The central government normally cannot convene arbakai because that is the purview of the jirgas. However, government officials can ask jirgas to form arbakai.[39] Indeed, there are several key principles for arbakai. First, leadership of the institution is collectively accepted. Second, the benefits and interests of all members of the tribe or community are equally shared. Third, tribe or community members are equally responsible for financial obligations and expenses.[40] Arbakai commanders are sometimes referred to by the Arabic term *ameer*, although others have called them arbakai *masher* or *kiftan*.[41] These leaders answer directly to the jirga.

---

[36] Tariq, *Tribal Security System*, p. 3.

[37] Masood Karokhail and Susanne Schmedil, *Integration of Traditional Structures into the State-Building Process: Lessons from the Tribal Liaison Office in Loya Paktia*, Kabul: Tribal Liaison Office, 2006, p. 63.

[38] Tariq, *Tribal Security System*, p. 3.

[39] Conrad Schetter, Raineer Glassner, and Massod Karokhail, *Understanding Local Violence, Security Arrangements in Kandahar, Kunduz and Paktia (Afghanistan)*, Bonn: University of Bonn, Center for Development Research, May 2006; Gregory Gajewski et al., "How War, a Tribal Social Structure and Donor Efforts Shape Institutional Change in Afghanistan: A Case Study of the Roads Sector," presented at the 2007 Conference of the European Association for Evolutionary Political Economy, Porto, Portugal, November 1–3, 2007.

[40] Tariq, *Tribal Security System*, p. 4.

[41] Miakhel, "The Importance of Tribal Structures and Pakhtunwali in Afghanistan," p. 1.

Selecting members for a given arbakai varies depending on the need.[42] In some cases, size is based on the principle of tsalweshtai (40): One out of every 40 men in a tribe is selected to serve in the arbakai. If a village has 800 men, it would contribute 20 to the arbakai.[43] In many cases, however, the size of the arbakai depends on the type of threat and the geographic area to be protected. The total can range from under a dozen to over 100 villagers, although there are rare exceptions where arbakai have temporarily grown to 400 or more.[44] Consequently, groups tend to be small and defensive, notably different from the warlord militias raised during the 1980s and 1990s, which grew to 50,000 part-time and full-time fighters.

Arbakai should not be conceived of in Western terms as an auxiliary paramilitary force. To begin with, the weight of community opinion is so strong that some arbakai are not even armed. Their power comes from the community, which can impose its will through informal law enforcement ranging from ostracism to house burning. For Pashtun communities, the traditional arbakai are also enforcers of tribal law, as well as security providers. In addition, their task of providing security to the community can mean avoiding violence. An arbakai may decide not to confront insurgents or criminals entering their territory with violence. Instead, the predisposition of the arbakai could be to engage and negotiate. If the insurgents agreed not to attack government forces in the arbakai territory (which would bring trouble to the community from government forces) and if they promised not to engage in other hostile or subversive acts, community leaders might let them pass unmolested. The key issue is to prevent harm to the community. If violence can be avoided by negotiating safe passage for transiting guerrillas, that could be the most prudent and preferable course of action.[45]

---

42 Tariq, *Tribal Security System*, p. 5; Karokhail and Schmeidl, *Integration of Traditional Structures*, p. 63.

43 Miakhel, "The Importance of Tribal Structures and Pakhtunwali in Afghanistan," p. 2.

44 Karokhail and Schmedil, *Integration of Traditional Structures*, p. 63.

45 Author interviews with Pashtun tribal leaders and former Taliban, Afghanistan, 2009.

Another key issue is *melmastia*. If travelers arrive peacefully and ask for food, water, and lodging, Pashtuns are bound by their tribal code to comply, even if the travelers are insurgents. Of course, Afghan and NATO officials might see it differently. They might view this accommodation as treason and might characterize the community as collaborators, subject to the house searches and nighttime raids that have contributed to popular support for the insurgency. Conversely, the arbakai's attitude might change if insurgents refused to negotiate and tried to collect taxes from the population, recruit young men, behead opponents, try to set up their own regime, and threaten the peace of the community.[46]

Arbakai are not a separate caste of warriors and are not professional soldiers. They are local villagers. Thus, the decision to fight in a given situation is likely to be pragmatic and cautious. Some have argued that arbakai are strongest in what is known as Loya Paktia, the southeastern region comprising the provinces of Paktia, Paktika, and Khowst.[47] "Due to the association with traditional structures, jirgas or shuras, *Arbakee* can only function in areas with strong and cohesive tribal structures," one study concludes:

> This at present is only true for the southeast of Afghanistan, and *Arbakee* are essentially unique to this area. Trying to copy the *Arbakee* model to other parts of Afghanistan where there is no history or experience with this concept, or paralleled strong tribal structures, may lead to an empowering of warlords and their militias.[48]

While the traditional tribal system has been weakened throughout Afghanistan and may not function in certain places, the tribal system does not exist only in Loya Paktia. There are Pashtun communities across southern and eastern Afghanistan, including ones in southern Afghan provinces, such as Kandahar, that use arbakai or similar local

---

[46] Author interviews with Pashtun tribal leaders and former Taliban, Afghanistan, 2009.

[47] Schmeidl and Karokhail, "The Role of Non-State Actors."

[48] Karokhail and Schmeidl, *Integration of Traditional Structures*, p. 63.

defense forces. Many Pashtun communities have some mechanism for bringing individuals together for self-defense and other communal tasks.

Conclusions

There is a strong tradition among Pashtuns for using arbakai and other policing forces to protect their villages. They tend to be small, defensive, confined to village-level protection, and controlled by the jirga or shura that called them. Our interviews with Afghan tribal and other community leaders indicate that arbakai and other similar institutions that are seen openly as directly controlled by the government may not enjoy local support and would probably not be effective. Part of the problem is that the central government is seen as corrupt and unable to provide security or basic services. Given this widespread antipathy toward the government, the jirgas or shuras may be reluctant to openly cooperate with it. In addition, public opinion polls suggest that the image of U.S. and Coalition forces is at its lowest point since 2001. Consequently, any jirga or shura calling for overt cooperation with what is increasingly seen as a foreign army of occupation may be counterproductive.[49]

---

[49] Author interviews with Pashtun tribal leaders and former Taliban, Afghanistan, April–May 2009.

CHAPTER FOUR

An Analysis of Community Policing

How effective have local defense forces been in Afghanistan and the region? Tribal and other local forces have been used throughout the history of Afghanistan and Pakistan, yet there is little systematic understanding of their effectiveness. In some cases, they have been effective in establishing order, as during the Musahiban dynasty. In other cases, they have contributed to instability, as in the early 1990s. But what factors have contributed to stability and instability? This chapter briefly examines the use of local forces since 1880. We argue that local forces have been most effective in establishing order when the central government remains the preponderant power (including national security forces); when local forces are developed through legitimate local institutions, such as jirgas and shuras; when the forces remain small and defensive; and when a quick-reaction force is available that can respond to an attack from insurgents or other outside forces. Table 4.1 briefly summarizes some local forces since 1880 in Afghanistan and Pakistan.

Local Forces from 1880 to 1978

Abdur Rahman Khan made one of the first attempts at modern state-building in Afghanistan and tried to establish an independent army. But he still relied on tribal forces in Pashtun areas of the country.[1] During his two-decade rule, the tribal forces were helpful in

---

[1] Dupree, *Afghanistan*, pp. 417–429.

Table 4.1
Examples of Tribal and Other Forces, 1880–Today

Case	Objective and Notes	Links to Central Government	Effectiveness
1880–1901 • Abdur Rahman Khan • Tribal forces, est. 40,000 • Pashtun areas of Afghanistan[a]	To establish order, with aid of army	Payments to tribal leaders	Fairly effective in establishing order, although Khan had to deal with several rebellions
1922–1936 • Waziristani forces, est. 10,000 • Waziristan	To secure Waziristan, with Pashtun forces and the regular British garrison in the agencies working together	Direct British payments to tribes	Effective in keeping relative peace for over a decade, but broke down in 1936 following rebellion led by the Faqir of Ipi
1929–1978 Musahiban dynasty • Arbakai, other local forces • Loya Paktia[b]	To establish order in Pashtun areas, including Loya Paktia	No direct salaries, but other forms of aid; central government gave privileged status, property, money, and exclusion from military service to tribal authorities	Effective in establishing security
1947–1948 • Pakistani lashkars, est. 2,000–5,000 • Kashmir	To seize Kashmir before the Maharaja of Jammu and Kashmir could exercise his legal right to join India after the British left in 1947	Organized by Pakistan General Akbar Khan and authorized by the Pakistan cabinet. Pakistan had loose command and control of tribal forces.	Not effective in securing Kashmir and minimally effective for offensive purposes. Lashkars did not hail from the areas in which they fought.

Table 4.1—Continued

Case	Objective and Notes	Links to Central Government	Effectiveness
1965 • Pakistani lashkars, est. <10,000–30,000ᶜ • Kashmir	To liberate Kashmir from Indian control	Trained and led by Pakistan Special Services Group, as well as Azad Kashmir and Jammu officers	Not effective in liberating Kashmir. Militants were defeated by regular Indian forces. They met either local hostility, indifference, or fear because of Indian reprisals.
1978–1979 • Lashkars, est. several hundred to several thousand • Pech Valley (Konar, Nuristan)	To revolt against the Afghan and Soviet governments	No links to the central government	Some effectiveness. Initially effective in organizing villages, but eventually usurped by Islamic resistance parties
1979–1989 • Mujahideen Anti-Soviet militias, est. 200,000–250,000 • Various locations throughout Afghanistan	To defeat the Soviet and Afghan armies	No link to central government. Some coordination by Pakistan's Directorate for Inter-Services Intelligence (ISI); received foreign funding and weapons	Effective in targeting the Soviet and Afghan armies
1984–1983 • Tribal and nontribal progovernment militias, est. 40,000 • Various locations throughout Afghanistan	To help establish order in rural areas of the country	Direct control of central government, mostly Ministry of Interior	Not effective during Soviet occupation due to unpopularity of the government. They were, however, better fighters than regular Afghan army.

Table 4.1—Continued

Case	Objective and Notes	Links to Central Government	Effectiveness
1980s to early 1990s • Hezb-i-Islami (Hekmatyar) militia, est., 60,000[d] • Eastern and southern Afghanistan	To overthrow the Soviet-backed government and establish order, especially in the east and south	None initially, except for with ISI; some efforts in early 1990s to coordinate via Afghan Interim Government	Effective in helping overthrow Soviet-backed government, but not effective in establishing order once Soviets departed
1980s to early 1990s • Jamiat-Islami (Rabbani) militia, est. 50,000–60,000[d] • Western and northern Afghanistan	To overthrow the Soviet-backed government and establish order, especially in the west and north	None initially, except for with ISI; some efforts in early 1990s to coordinate via Afghan Interim Government	Effective in helping overthrow Soviet-backed government, but not effective in establishing order once Soviets departed
1980s to early 1990s • Ittehadi-Islami (Sayyaf) militia, est. 40,000–50,000[d] • Eastern and northern Afghanistan	To overthrow the Soviet-backed government and establish order, especially in the east and north	None initially, except for with ISI; some efforts in early 1990s to coordinate via Afghan Interim Government	Effective in helping overthrow Soviet-backed government, but not effective in establishing order once Soviets departed
1980s to early 1990s • Hezb-i-Islami (Khalis) militia, est. 40,000[d] • Eastern Afghanistan	To overthrow the Soviet-backed government and establish order, especially in such key areas as the Kabul-Jalalabad corridor	None initially, except for with ISI; some efforts in early 1990s to coordinate via Afghan Interim Government	Effective in helping overthrow Soviet-backed government, but not effective in establishing order once Soviets departed

Table 4.1—Continued

Case	Objective and Notes	Links to Central Government	Effectiveness
1980s to early 1990s • Harakat-Inqilabi-Islami (Nabi) militia, est. 30,000–40,000[d] • Western and southern Afghanistan	To overthrow the Soviet-backed government and establish order, especially in the west and south	None initially, except for with ISI; some efforts in early 1990s to coordinate via Afghan Interim Government	Effective in helping overthrow Soviet-backed government, but not effective in establishing order once Soviets departed
1980s to early 1990s • Mahazi-Milli-Islam (Gailani) militia, est. 30,000–40,000[d] • Southern Afghanistan	To overthrow the Soviet-backed government and establish order, especially in the south	None initially, except for with ISI; some efforts in early 1990s to coordinate via Afghan Interim Government	Effective in helping overthrow Soviet-backed government, but not effective in establishing order once Soviets departed
1980s to early 1990s • Jabhai-Nijati-Milli-Afghanistan (Mojadeddi) militia, est. 20,000–30,000[d] • Southern Afghanistan	To overthrow the Soviet-backed government and establish order, especially in the south	None initially, except for with ISI; some efforts in early 1990s to coordinate via Afghan Interim Government	Effective in helping overthrow Soviet-backed government, but not effective in establishing order once Soviets departed
1980s to early 1990s • Abdul Rashid Dostum's Jowzjani militia, est. 40,000[d] • Northern Afghanistan	To establish control in various areas of the north	None	Effective in establishing control of various regions in the north, but contributed to onset of civil war in 1990s

Table 4.1—Continued

Case	Objective and Notes	Links to Central Government	Effectiveness
2001–2002 • Anti-Taliban and anti-al Qa'ida forces, several dozen to tens of thousands • Multiple places across Afghanistan	To overthrow the Taliban government and capture or kill al Qa'ida fighters	Direct links with U.S. forces operating in Afghanistan	Initially effective in overthrowing Taliban government, but became unpopular after war
2006–2008 • Afghan National Auxiliary Police, est. 5,000 to 10,000 • Helmand, Zabol, Kandahar, Farah, Oruzgan, Ghazni	To help ANA, ANP, and Coalition forces establish order in rural areas	Payment, training, and uniforms through central government and United States	Not effective, partly because they were never integrated into local tribal and community structures
2008–2009 • Bajaur, Swat, Dir and Buner lashkars, est. several thousand • Salarzai lashkars, perhaps up to 30,000 • NWFP, Pakistan	To establish static checkpoints and improve road security in conjunction with Pakistan Frontier Corps and Army operations	ISI and Ministry of Interior helped organize	Some effectiveness

Table 4.1—Continued

Case	Objective and Notes	Links to Central Government	Effectiveness
2008– • Afghanistan Public Protection Program, est. roughly 1,200 • Wardak	To establish security in Wardak	Payment, training, and uniforms through central government and United States	Some effectiveness in establishing security in Wardak

NOTE: *Tribal forces* are defined as those organized through the traditional tribal system; *non-tribal forces* are those organized by non-traditional means, such as mujahideen political parties, warlords, or government agencies. While both types of forces may include tribesmen, the organizing principles and motivations are fundamentally different.

[a] This includes the north.

[b] Loya Paktia consists of Paktia, Khowst, Paktika provinces.

[c] As many as 30,000 assembled, although probably fewer than 10,000 were used.

[d] These were the force sizes in 1990.

establishing order, although he still faced armed opposition from Hazaras, Aimaqs, Nuristanis, and various Pashtun tribal confederations throughout the country.[2] But some subsequent Afghan governments went too far. Amanullah Khan, who ruled Afghanistan from 1919 to 1929, tried to create a strong central state in the image of Ataturk's Turkey and Reza Shah's Iran. This proved disastrous. The central government's attempt to push into rural areas sparked social and political revolts, first in Khowst in 1923 and then in Jalalabad in 1928. By 1929, local rebellions became so serious that Amanullah was forced to abdicate, and Afghanistan deteriorated into several months of anarchy.

Pakistan also has a rich history of using local tribal institutions. The British established Pashtun forces to secure Waziristan beginning in 1922, when London overruled the government of India and put a permanent military garrison inside Waziristan. The British garrison of 15,000 soldiers was supported by 10,000 Pashtun tribal warriors. The tribal force was deployed to patrol major roadways and respond to insurrections, and the British paid the tribes as an incentive to refrain from rebellion. The tribal force was fairly effective in helping establish order for over a decade. It developed a close relationship with local Waziri tribes, including their leaders, and was used largely for defensive purposes. But the pro-British tribal force ultimately broke down in 1936 following a rebellion led by the Faqir of Ipi.[3]

In addition, the newly formed Pakistan state used lashkars in 1947 in an effort to seize Kashmir before the Maharaja of Jammu and Kashmir could join India. Most were from the Mahsud, Afridi, and Mohmand tribes, though there were also some Muslim Kashmiri auxiliaries. Pakistan General Akbar Khan organized the forces and had loose command and control. Ultimately, however, the lashkars were not effective. They did not succeed in seizing Kashmir because they faced a much better organized Indian army and because many of the lashkar fighters were not from the areas they fought in, undermining

---

[2]   Kristian Berg Harpviken, "Transcending Traditionalism: The Emergence of Non-State Military Formations in Afghanistan," *Journal of Peace Research*, Vol. 34, No. 3, August 1997; Rubin, *The Fragmentation of Afghanistan*, pp. 48–52.

[3]   Warren, "'Bullocks Treading Down Wasps'?"

their legitimacy.[4] Pakistan also used lashkars during Operation Gibraltar in 1965 to liberate Kashmir from Indian control. They were trained and led by Pakistan's Special Services Group and by Azad Kashmir and Jammu officers. Much as in 1947, however, they were ineffective. The locals viewed the lashkars as illegitimate because most, if not all, the commanders spoke no Kashmiri.[5] In the end, the lashkars fell to regular Indian forces. In both the 1947 and 1965 cases, tribal lashkars were used with little success for prolonged offensive operations against much better equipped and organized armies.

Beginning in 1929, Afghanistan enjoyed an unprecedented period of stability under the leadership of Nadir Shah and his successors, especially Zahir Shah and Daoud Khan. Some scholars refer to this period as the Musahiban dynasty (based on the lineage name), and the Musahibans were Durrani Pashtun.[6] Nadir Shah assembled a tribal army to capture Kabul from Habibullah Kalakani in 1929 and used tribal forces against an uprising by the Shinwari tribes of the south and Tajiks in Kabul. As the anthropologist Louis Dupree argued, "conservative tribal and religious leaders were one of the foundations of power" during this period.[7]

The Musahibans built strong central government security forces, including an Afghan army. By 1933, Nadir Shah had established a modern army of 70,000 soldiers, with professional officer education and a noncommissioned officer corps. By 1945, the army had grown

---

[4] Shuja Nawaz, *Crossed Swords: Pakistan, Its Army, and the Wars Within*, New York: Oxford University Press, 2008, pp. 42–75; Julian Schofield and Reeta Tremblay, "Why Pakistan Failed: Tribal Focoism in Kashmir," *Small Wars and Insurgencies*, Vol. 19, No. 1, March 2008, pp. 23–38.

[5] Altaf Gauhar, *Ayub Khan: Pakistan's First Military Ruler*, Lahore: Sang-e-Meel Publications, 1993; Schofield and Tremblay, "Why Pakistan Failed"; Nawaz, *Crossed Swords*, pp. 205–214.

[6] On the Musahiban dynasty, see Thomas Barfield, *Afghanistan: A Cultural and Political History*, Princeton, N.J.: Princeton University Press, 2010, pp. 195–225.

[7] Dupree, *Afghanistan*, p. 460.

to 110,000 and eventually included an 8,000-man air force.[8] These forces were occasionally used to crush revolts and mediate inter- and intratribal disputes. In 1959 and 1960, for instance, Daoud Khan used the Afghan army to settle fighting between the Mangals and Zadrans in eastern Afghanistan. He also deployed the army to Kandahar in December 1959 to crush a riot over increased government taxes.[9]

Overall, arbakai and other local forces were effective in establishing order, though they did face some resistance from Uzbeks, Tajiks, and Hazaras.[10] The central government also encouraged local customary law to help establish order. As one study concludes, during the Zahir Shah and Daoud Khan years:

> the state used these systems as a form of indirect rule in areas where they lacked the administrative capacity to rule directly. It proved very useful for local government officials to rely on the informal system to maintain general peace and order.[11]

The government exempted tribes in Loya Paktia from conscription into the military and police forces. Tribal jirgas there used arbakai as police to implement their decisions or to respond to specific threats against the community or tribe. Each major tribe in Loya Paktia—such as the Jaji, Mangal, and Zadran—had one leader supervising the arbakai.[12] The government often did not provide direct salaries to the arbakai in Loya Paktia but instead gave the tribal authorities privileged status, property, money, advisory roles, and exclusion from military service.

The Zahir Shah government used Shinwari, Mohmand, and Khogyani arbakai to establish order in eastern Afghanistan in the 1960s

---

8   Obaid Younossi, Peter Dahl Thruelsen, Jonathan Vaccaro, Jerry M. Sollinger, and Brian Grady, *The Long March: Building an Afghan National Army*, Santa Monica, Calif.: RAND Corporation, MG-845-RDCC/OSD, 2009, p. 5.

9   Dupree, *Afghanistan*, pp. 534–538.

10   Rubin, *The Fragmentation of Afghanistan*, pp. 58–59.

11   Barfield, "Culture and Custom," p. 360. Also see Thomas J. Barfield, "Weak Links on a Rusty Chain: Structural Weaknesses in Afghanistan's Provincial Government Administration," in Shahrani and Canfield, eds. *Revolutions and Rebellions*, 1984, pp. 170–183.

12   Miakhel, "The Importance of Tribal Structures and Pakhtunwali in Afghanistan."

and 1970s. The government handed over a section of irrigated land to each tribal jirga, which was intended to help cover arbakai expenses. In some cases, the amount of land ranged from 1 km^2 per small village with one or two arbakai members to 8 km^2 for larger arbakai.[13] Unlike the previous Pakistan lashkars, these arbakai were used primarily for defense and were organized under the auspices of legitimate tribal institutions, contributing to their effectiveness. In Nuristan, villages established local defense forces to protect their areas. As one assessment of the Vaygal Valley of south-central Nuristan concluded, "[t]he survival of Kalasha villages depended on careful, unrelenting attention to defensive arrangements," since there was virtually no government presence in the area.[14]

In sum, the Musahiban dynasty, which included Zahir Shah, Nadir Shah, and Daoud Khan, ruled Afghanistan from 1929 to 1978. It was one of the most stable periods in modern Afghan history, partly because the Musahibans understood the importance of local power. Security was established using a combination of top-down efforts by the central government (especially in urban areas) and bottom-up efforts by local tribes and other communities (especially in rural areas). As anthropologist Thomas Barfield concluded,

> Political stability in rural Afghanistan under the Musahibans rested on the tacit recognition of two distinct power structures: the provincial and subprovincial administrations, which were arms of the central government, and tribal or village structures indigenous to each region. While the central government had been effective in expanding its power into the countryside, its goals were limited to encapsulating local political structures in order to prevent them from causing trouble. It never attempted to displace or transform the deep-rooted social organizations in which most people lived out their lives.[15]

---

[13] Tariq, *Tribal Security System*, p. 9.

[14] David J. Katz, "Responses to Central Authority in Nuristan: The Case of the Vaygal Valley Kalasha," in Shahrani and Canfield, eds. *Revolutions and Rebellions*, 1984, pp. 97, 99.

[15] Barfield, *Afghanistan*, p. 220.

Local Forces During the War Years

Over the next two decades of war, government institutions stopped functioning in some areas of the country, and a new cadre of military commanders emerged. Beginning in 1978, tribes in the Pech Valley of eastern Afghanistan formed lashkars to revolt against the Soviet-backed Afghan government. They were initially effective in organizing villages to protect themselves, although they faced deep resistance from government-backed tribal forces and were eventually usurped by Islamic resistance groups.[16] The power and influence of the Islamic clergy (ulema) also rose sharply, including the right to administer religious law (sharia) in non-Pashtun areas, where there was little central authority.

By the time the Soviets invaded in 1979, a range of anti-Soviet and progovernment forces had been established throughout the country. Some were tribal forces, while others—such as Abdul Rashid Dostum's Jowzjani militia—were centered on charismatic, powerful commanders.[17] There were some successful uses of arbakai during the Soviet era. In several Afghan refugee camps in the Haripur area of Pakistan's North West Frontier Province (NWFP), for instance, arbakais were raised among the refugees. These groups of unpaid volunteers worked effectively to maintain law and order, discourage harassment of girls, and prevent theft.[18] The Soviets attempted to establish a range of tribal forces, mostly under direct control of the Afghan Ministry of Interior and officially sanctioned in March 1983 by a jirga in Kabul.[19] These forces were not particularly effective, partly because the Afghan government was so illegitimate and partly because the government

---

[16] David B. Edwards, *Before Taliban: Genealogies of the Afghan Jihad*, Berkeley, Calif.: University of California Press, 2002, p. 164.

[17] Abdulkader H. Sinno, *Organizations at War in Afghanistan and Beyond*, Ithaca, N.Y.: Cornell University Press, 2008, pp. 124–126.

[18] Tariq, *Tribal Security System*, pp. 8–9.

[19] Giustozzi, *Empires of Mud*, pp. 53–68.

tried to control them from the center.[20] After Soviet troops left, tribal and nontribal forces helped keep the communist regime in power for three years. The strategy failed when the Soviet food and budget subsidy was cut, and it became clear that the central government in Kabul had lost both foreign and domestic support.

Critics of civilian defense forces often cite the Soviet case as evidence of their unreliability. But this reflects a misunderstanding of the situation, since the Soviets created large, offensive forces under the control of such commanders as Abdul Rashid Dostum. These forces were veritable *militias*, not the community policing forces that the Musahibans worked with. In addition, each of the main mujahideen parties fighting the communists had fairly large militias, but all should be seen as fundamentally different from traditional Pashtun local defense forces. Each force consisted of tens of thousands of part- or full-time fighters:

- Hezb-i-Islami (Hekmatyar): 60,000
- Jamiat-i Islami: 50,000–60,000
- Ittehadi-Islami: 40,000–50,000
- Hezb-i-Islami (Khalis): 40,000
- Harakati-Inqilabi-Islami: 30,000–40,000
- Mahazi-Milli-Islam: 30,000–40,000
- Jabhai-Nijati-Milli-Afghanistan: 20,000–30,000.[21]

These forces helped drive Soviet forces out of Afghanistan. But the subsequent collapse of the Afghan government paved the way for the rise of warlords. As Antonio Giustozzi concludes in his assessment of warlords in Afghanistan:

---

[20] Richard F. Nyrop and Donald M. Seekins, eds., "National Security," Afghanistan Country Study, Washington, D.C.: The American University, Foreign Area Studies, 1986; Lester W. Grau and Michael A. Gress, *The Soviet-Afghan War: How a Superpower Fought and Lost*, Lawrence, Kan.: University Press of Kansas, 2002, pp. 50–51; Allan Orr, "Recasting Afghan Strategy," *Small Wars and Insurgencies*, Vol. 20, No. 1, March 2009.

[21] Zalmay Khalilzad, *Prospects for the Afghan Interim Government*, Santa Monica, Calif.: RAND Corporation, R-3949, 1991; Olivier Roy, *Islam and Resistance in Afghanistan*, 2nd ed., New York: Cambridge University Press, 1990.

From the very beginning both the Mujaddidi and the Rab-
bani governments appeared very weak and unable to control
Afghanistan . . . . A key step that contributed to the emergence
of warlordism and to the onset of the civil war was Minister of
Defense Massud's decision de facto to abandon the armed forces
inherited from Najibullah.[22]

Without *any* central government forces that could control or provide
oversight to local defense forces, Afghanistan slipped into anarchy.
Warlord militias multiplied across the country. Examples are Rasul
Pahlawan in Faryab; Ghaffar Pahlawan in Sar-i Pul; Jaffar Naderi in
Baghlan; Esmatullah Muslim in Kandahar; Ismail Khan in Herat;
Gulbuddin Hekmatyar's Hezb-i-Islami in Lowgar and other areas;
Massoud's Jami'at-i Islami in Panjshir and other areas; and Abdul
Rashid Dostum's Junbesh-i Milli-ye Islami in Balkh, Jowzjan, and
other northern provinces.

Local militias established their own power bases through several
sources of revenue, such as drug money, land taxes (*ushr*), taxes on
goods, and foreign aid.[23] Many of these groups turned on each other
in a bid to control Kabul, creating a window of opportunity for the
Taliban to rise in 1994. Primary source accounts indicate that disparate
militia forces began to emerge as the state disintegrated. "The roads [in
Kandahar] were full of checkpoints," noted Abdul Salam Zaeef, who
was in Kandahar Province in the early 1990s and eventually became
the Taliban ambassador to Pakistan. "Every few kilometers a different
gang or commander demanded money or goods. Even nowadays when
people talk about that time, they call it *topakiyaan*. The time of the men
with guns."[24] Ultimately, these forces could not establish order effectively because they centered on charismatic individuals rather than on
legitimate tribal institutions. They also became excessively large and
well armed, were used for offensive operations, and operated in a governance vacuum because the government had stopped functioning.

---

22 Giustozzi, *Empires of Mud*, p. 71.

23 Giustozzi, *Empires of Mud*.

24 Abdul Salam Zaeef, *My Life with the Taliban*, New York: Hurst & Company, 2010, p. 59.

During the Taliban years, there was a specific effort to coerce or co-opt Pashtun tribal and other local leaders.[25]

After the September 11, 2001, terrorist attacks, the Central Intelligence Agency and U.S. Special Forces worked with a range of tribal and other local forces to overthrow the Taliban government. Some centered on individuals, such as Pasha Khan Zadran, while others centered on Pashtun tribes, such as the Popalzai and Barakzai. In parts of the east, for example, local forces "led every mounted patrol and most major operations," partly because, according to one U.S. military assessment, "they knew the ground better and could more easily spot something that was out of place or suspicious."[26] Such forces were often used for the outer perimeters of cordon-and-search operations. In several operations, such as the Battle of Deh Chopan, militia forces were used to provide intelligence and the bulk of the maneuver force.[27] In the west, U.S. forces provided assistance to Ismail Khan, which allowed him to establish significant political and fiscal autonomy in Herat Province. He controlled military and civil administration there, supported by foreign aid, road taxes, and customs duties from trade with Iran, Turkmenistan, and other Afghan provinces.[28] In the south, U.S. forces provided money and arms to Gul Agha Shirzai and other warlords to help target al Qa'ida operatives.[29]

---

[25] See, for example, Robert D. Crews and Amin Tarzi, eds., *The Taliban and the Crisis of Afghanistan*, Cambridge, Mass.: Harvard University Press, 2008; Mohammad Osman Tariq Elias, "The Resurgence of the Taliban in Kabul: Logar and Wardak," in Giustozzi, ed., *Decoding the New Taliban*, 2009, p. 45.

[26] David L. Buffaloe, *Conventional Forces in Low-Intensity Conflict: The 82d Airborne in Firebase Shkin*, Arlington, Va.: Association of the United States Army, Landpower Essay 04-2, 2004, p. 12.

[27] On a first-hand account of the Battle for Deh Chopan, see Michael McInerney, "The Battle for Deh Chopan, Part 1," *Soldier of Fortune*, August 2004; Michael McInerney, "The Battle for Deh Chopan, Part 2," *Soldier of Fortune*, September 2004.

[28] Anne Evans, Nick Manning, Yasin Osmani, Anne Tully, and Andrew Wilder, *A Guide to Government in Afghanistan*, Washington, D.C.: World Bank, 2004, p. 14; Giustozzi, *Empires of Mud*, pp. 233–238.

[29] On warlords and Afghanistan, see A. M. Roe, "To Create a Stable Afghanistan: Provisional Reconstruction Teams, Good Governance, and a Splash of History," *Military Review*, Vol. 85, No. 6, 2005; Government of Afghanistan, *Security Sector Reform: Disbandment of*

U.S. assistance to warlords—especially when it did not go through legitimate local or national institutions—weakened the effort to rebuild a central government and became deeply unpopular for many Afghans. One poll conducted for the U.S. military concluded that "a high percentage of respondents identified local commanders as bringers of insecurity to their district."[30] According to the Afghanistan National Security Council's *National Threat Assessment*:

> Non-statutory armed forces and their commanders pose a direct threat to the national security of Afghanistan. They are the principal obstacle to the expansion of the rule of law into the provinces and thus the achievement of the social economic goals that the people of Afghanistan and their Government, supported by the International Community, wish to deliver.[31]

In 2006, the Afghan government and Combined Security Transition Command–Afghanistan came up with a plan to build what became known as the Afghan National Auxiliary Police. "There were not enough guns and people to protect local villagers," remarked Ambassador Ronald Neumann. "This is counterinsurgency 101: to protect the local population."[32] In February 2006, senior officials from the Afghan Ministry of Interior and Ministry of Finance approached Ambassador Neumann and MG Robert Durbin. The Afghans wanted to hire an additional 200 to 400 police per district. The idea was to create a new force, which would eventually be called the Afghan National Auxiliary Police. Durbin and his deputy, Canadian BGen Gary O'Brien, briefed

---

Illegal Armed Groups Programme (DIAG) and Disarmament, Demobilisation, and Reintegration Programme (DDR), Kabul, October 2005; Mark Sedra, *Challenging the Warlord Culture: Security Sector Reform in Post-Taliban Afghanistan*, Bonn: Bonn International Center for Conversion, 2002.

[30] Combined Forces Command–Afghanistan and Altai Consulting, *Afghan National Development Poll*, Kabul, 2005.

[31] Afghanistan National Security Council, *National Threat Assessment*, Kabul, 2005, p. 3. Also see Afghanistan Ministry of Defense, *The National Military Strategy*, Kabul, October 2005.

[32] Author interview with Ambassador Ronald Neumann, September 7, 2007.

Neumann on the initial concept in the spring of 2006, and Durbin then briefed President Karzai in May 2006. His plan was to establish a "mercenary" police force designed to fill a local gap in Afghan security forces.[33] The auxiliary police program meant training villagers for ten days and equipping them with guns. They were then sent to secure static checkpoints and conduct operations with Coalition forces against insurgents in six unstable provinces: Helmand, Zabol, Kandahar, Farah, Oruzgan, and Ghazni.[34] But the Afghan National Auxiliary Police was ultimately unsuccessful. It was never integrated into legitimate local institutions, including jirgas and shuras, and local Afghans never considered it legitimate.

In addition, the Pakistan military supported the creation of lashkars. In 2009, for example, a grand jirga in Kala Dhaka raised two lashkars to stop the infiltration of fleeing militants from Buner and Swat and to keep watch on the movement of internally displaced persons. "The peace and harmony of the area is dear to all the five tribes and, if needed, the Lashkars will take up arms against the militants," declared the elders in a public statement.[35] Another news report announced the creation of the Pakhtun Aman Lashkar (PAL) to fight militants in Swat, Buner, and Dir. The organizer, Syed Kamal Shah, a former NWFP minister, proclaimed:

> Pahktuns have no escape from the Taliban but to rise against this menace. There is no other way out but a Lashkar uprising. The PAL would be a force on the back of these local Lashkars and we would see to it that the Taliban are identified and eliminated wherever they operate in these three districts and the FATA [Federally Administered Tribal Areas].[36]

---

[33] Author interview with Major General Robert Durbin, January 3, 2008.

[34] Author interview with Ambassador Ronald Neumann, September 7, 2007.

[35] "Pakistan: Volunteer Forces Raised to Stop Militants from Entering Manshera, NWFP," *The News Online* (Pakistan), May 29, 2009.

[36] "Pakistan: Local Paramilitary Force to be Launched to Fight Taliban in NWFP," *The News Online* (Pakistan), May 28, 2009.

There were some successes, notably the 4,000-man Salarzai tribal lashkar in Bajaur in 2008.[37] When militants invaded Buner District in April 2009, a local *khan* organized a lashkar to stop them. But the lashkar was destroyed. In December 2008, Pir Samiullah organized a lashkar against militants in Swat. Militants captured him and eight of his supporters and executed them publicly.[38] In Bajaur, local militants retaliated for the success of the Salarzai lashkar with a series of suicide bombings and assassinations. The latter included slitting the throats of four Hilal Khel tribal leaders from the Charmang area of Bajaur who had organized a lashkar against militants, dumping their bodies by the side of the road.[39]

One of the most devastating reprisals occurred in Orakzai District of NWFP on October 10, 2008. Militants targeted a jirga, attended by hundreds of tribal leaders, who had decided to oppose them and had formed a lashkar. The truck bomb killed over one hundred people and effectively destroyed the lashkar.[40] A common thread running through these examples is the lack of adequate government support. In each case, the Pakistani government encouraged community resistance to local militants. But these efforts were not followed up with effective communication networks to call for help or a military quick-reaction force to aid a tribal lashkar under attack. The psychological effect of these reprisals led to a reluctance among Pashtun tribes in Pakistan to confront insurgent groups and a sense of betrayal that the government let them down.

This situation has changed since the Pakistan army began its offensive against the Taliban in Swat and neighboring districts in the spring of 2009. The military campaign displaced as many as two million people in the NWFP and FATA and sent a clear signal that

---

[37] Zahid Hussain, "Pakistan Turns to Tribal Militias," *Wall Street Journal*, September 30, 2008.

[38] Hussain, "Pakistan Turns to Tribal Militias."

[39] Jane Perlez and Pir Zubair Shah, "Pakistan Uses Tribal Militias in Taliban War," *New York Times*, October 24, 2008.

[40] Jason Motlaugh, "Pakistan's Use of Tribal Militias to Target Taliban Yields Mixed Results," *U.S. News & World Report*, December 5, 2008.

the Pakistani military would target Islamic insurgents in some frontier areas. That campaign was followed up by other operations in the intervening period, culminating in the 2010 capture in Pakistan of the Afghan Taliban's most important commander, Mullah Berader, who had previously operated with impunity in Pakistani territory. As a consequence, there are many reports of lashkars being formed again to pursue the fleeing Taliban in various tribal communities or to make sure they do not come back. Now that they have Pakistani military support, Pashtun communities are willing to confront the insurgents openly in ways they avoided only a year ago.

Conclusions

Local defense forces have been used in many wars and counterinsurgencies, including those in Afghanistan. As Frank Kitson has argued, counterinsurgency is labor intensive, and the recruitment of defensive, community-policing forces is often essential to enable an overstretched army and police to focus on offensive operations against the insurgents.[41] Local defense forces—often referred to as civilian defense forces, home guards, and self-defense patrols—have often been critical for governments to defeat insurgents. They have been effective in a wide variety of counterinsurgencies, including those in Iraq, Malaysia, Oman, Greece, the Philippines, Peru, Guatemala, Colombia, and even the United States during the war of independence against the British.[42] Critics may charge that relying on undisciplined civilians who may have their own agendas inevitably leads to abuses. This concern is valid, but it overlooks the plethora of occasions when these forces, regardless of their shortcomings, played a key role in maintaining government authority in violent areas.

In Guatemala, for example, under the 1982 Beans and Bullets campaign of General Efraín Rios Montt, able-bodied men in West-

---

[41] Frank Kitson, *Bunch of Five*, London: Faber, 1977.

[42] See, for example, George Washington's use of militias during the American Revolution in Douglas Southall Freeman, *Washington*, New York: Simon and Schuster, 1968.

ern Highlands Indian communities were expected to join "self-defense patrols." Service in these patrols was often on a rotating basis. By enlisting all the able-bodied men, the Guatemalan army helped turn entire villages against the guerrillas. The army handed out rifles to the Indians and provided training and ammunition. No one was paid a salary because this was considered community service. Instead of individual payments, villages that formed self-defense patrols received development projects and other assistance from the government. While the guerrillas proclaimed that they were organizing the people against the repression of the oligarchy, the Guatemalan military did a better job of organizing local Indians against the insurgency. At the peak of the program, the Guatemalan civil defense forces comprised 350,000 Indians under arms, by some estimates. The program was so successful that it broke the back of the communist insurgency and stopped the insurgent effort to take control of the Western Highlands.

In the United States, irregulars were used during the American Revolution and Civil War.[43] In Algeria, the French raised *harkis*, lightly armed irregulars recruited to provide security in local villages and towns throughout Algeria. These were supplemented by *groupes d'auto-défence* (self-defense groups) armed and trained by French forces and tasked with providing local security.[44] In Oman, local forces were combined with civic action teams to turn the population against insurgents. In Vietnam, civilian defense forces were also implemented, both by the Americans and the French. These efforts were generally successful in establishing security as long as they were limited to protecting the villages in which the armed civilians resided. Too often, however, these units began to be treated as auxiliaries of regular forces and were sent on campaigns outside their villages, where they did not perform well. This lesson continues to be relevant in Afghanistan today.

---

[43] Freeman, *Washington*; John J. Tierney, Jr., *Chasing Ghosts: Unconventional Warfare in American History*, Washington, D.C.: Potomac Books, 2007.

[44] Geraint Hughes and Christian Tripodi, "Anatomy of a Surrogate: Historical Precedents and Implications for Contemporary Counter-Insurgency and Counter-Terrorism," *Small Wars & Insurgencies*, Vol. 20, No. 1, March 2009.

Afghanistan's own history suggests several lessons about the use of local forces. First, central government forces need a preponderance of power. The Musahibans relied on a strong Afghan army to crush revolts and mediate inter- and intratribal disputes in Pashtun areas. But the disintegration of the national army in 1992 created a window of opportunity for the rise of warlords, whose power was unchecked. Second, Afghan local forces—such as arbakai—have been most successful when developed through legitimate institutions, such as village-level jirgas and shuras. The use of the local institutions ensures the legitimacy of the forces. Forces under the control of warlords, as in the 1980s and early 1990s, have generally been unpopular because they are used to benefit individuals rather than communities. Third, local forces should be small, defensive, and used primarily for village-level security. Lashkars and other forces used for offensive purposes to seize territory, as in Pakistan in 1947 and 1965, have often been unsuccessful. Fourth, a quick-reaction force is vital to assist local forces that come under attack. One of the most striking lessons from the lashkars in Bajaur was the Pakistan government's failure to protect them when they came under attack from militants, who tried to assassinate key tribal leaders and lashkar members.

CHAPTER FIVE

Organizing Local Defense Forces

We define a *local defense force* as a traditional, community-based group composed of local civilians who police their own communities against insurgents and criminals. They are small, village-level, defensive, and under the control of local shuras or jirgas. In many cases, these patrols should be organized within the existing tribal system. Where the tribal system has broken down, the Afghan government should work with the legitimate local institutions to establish local defense forces.

Although a primary function of arbakai and similar institutions is community policing, their members are not generally full-time policemen and do not have the legal powers of government law enforcement officers. But they do enforce tribal or community law. In general, their duties should be defensive, focused on patrolling their own localities. Local defense forces are not meant to be auxiliaries for military units seeking to engage enemy forces, although this point should not preclude some members serving as guides, informants, or providing other services. But past efforts to use local forces as offensive paramilitary auxiliaries have not been successful.

One size does not fit all. It would be imprudent to take a single approach to raising local defense forces in Afghanistan. The tribal structure has evolved differently throughout Afghanistan and may not exist at all in certain areas. Any concerted effort must be adaptable to local conditions, especially the consensus of the jirgas and shuras in the affected villages and districts. Any local defense force program should be established in accordance with a comprehensive counterinsurgency strategy that addresses diverse psychological, social, economic, political, and security concerns across Afghanistan.[1] While this document focuses on bottom-up security measures, other economic, justice, and development efforts are also critical to long-term security and stability.

The weakness of the Taliban and other insurgent groups at the grassroots level creates a powerful impetus to establish a more-comprehensive bottom-up strategy. Public opinion polls, for example, continue to show that support for the Taliban is low, even in comparison to that for the Afghan government. In fact, when asked, "who would you rather have ruling Afghanistan today: the current government or the Taliban," one recent poll found that 90 percent of Afghans said they would have the current government rule, and only 6 percent said the Taliban.[2]

By 2010, a growing number of communities had begun to mobilize against insurgents. In Arghandab District, Kandahar Province, Alikozais revolted against the Taliban and established local defense forces to protect their own villages, with the support of the Afghan National Police and NATO forces. In Shindand District, Herat Province, local Noorzais mobilized against insurgents in the Zer-e Koh Valley. In May, a local force in Parmakan Village fought off local Taliban with assistance from Afghan Army commandos and U.S. Special Operations Forces (SOF). In Gizab District, Day Kundi Province, Hazara and Pashtun communities successfully resisted insurgents and reached out to the Afghan government for assistance. In Khakrez District, Kandahar Province, local forces established an expanding security zone in the district center with the help of Afghan and NATO forces. In Paktia Province, Jaji, Chamkani, Moqbil, and Mangal tribes created local defense forces to protect themselves against insurgents in such districts as Chamkani and Jani Kheyl, with the aid of the Afghan government and NATO. In all these areas, which the authors visited, local communities protected their populations, reintegrated insurgents, increased development with help from Afghan and international agencies, and established a better connection with the Afghan government.

---

1 On local strategies, also see Thomas H. Johnson and M. Chris Mason, "All Counterinsurgency Is Local," *The Atlantic*, Vol. 302, No. 3, October 2008.

2 ABC, BBC, and ARD, "Afghanistan: Where Things Stand," poll, January 2010, p. 20.

In June 2009, Afghan and NATO officials established the Community Defense Initiative—later renamed the Local Defense Initiative and then the Village Stability Platform—to leverage local communities that had already resisted the Taliban or other insurgent groups. This grassroots program aimed to help communities build village-level, defensive police forces under the control of legitimate jirgas and shuras and to provide development aid to participating villages. By late 2010, several communities showed promising signs of improving security, especially in southern Afghanistan. They established effective local forces that secured their villages, repelled insurgents, and developed a good relationship with the Afghan government. The lessons learned during the creation—and expansion—of the Village Stability Platform informed this chapter.

The historical use of local security forces and the current realities in Afghanistan suggest organizing a local defense strategy around the following principles: building strong national army and police forces that retain the preponderance of power, identifying grassroots initiatives, utilizing legitimate local institutions, providing quick-reaction forces to aid endangered communities, establishing development assistance to communities, and developing psychological operations.

National Preponderance of Power

One of the starkest lessons from the early 1990s is the inherent problem of pursuing a bottom-up strategy without competent central government forces. Afghanistan Minister of Defense Ahmed Shah Massoud's de facto decision in 1992 to abandon a strong central army increased the anarchy already emerging in Afghanistan. In contrast, the Musahibans pursued an effective bottom-up strategy with a strong national army, which retained a preponderance of power. The lesson is clear. Developing a successful bottom-up strategy *requires* building competent national army and police forces that retain a preponderance of power, which can crush revolts, conduct offensive actions against militants, and help adjudicate any inter- and intratribal disputes that might occur.

In addition, any local defense program must be Afghan-led. Some Afghans oppose large, overt foreign military footprints.[3] Taliban propaganda consistently refers to the current war as one of foreign occupation. One Taliban propaganda message warned Afghans that

> the Americans themselves have unveiled their antagonistic nature toward the Afghans, and disclosed their ill-fated objectives considering the killing of the Afghans, burning them in more furnaces of war, and torturing them as a U.S. duty and main course of action.[4]

The population must perceive that its local defense force is protecting local interests, that the local jirga or shura has organized it, and that it is not beholden to any outsiders.

Nonetheless, the Afghan government can—and should—provide the resources and capabilities to support local defense programs. This could be done in several ways. Provincial governors and district subgovernors can participate in local shuras and jirgas to help oversee the program and provide assistance when they are able to. Their role may be particularly important for local defense programs in areas with multiple tribes to assist in mediation efforts. For example, a number of tribes in Chamkani District in Paktia Province, including the Jajis, Chamkanis, Mangals, and Moqbils, have opposed the Taliban and other insurgents. But they have engaged in land and other disputes with each other. In addition, ANA and ANP forces should be involved in helping vet community defense members, train them in basic defensive tactics, share information with them, and establish a community system that can respond in emergencies.

Avoiding the appearance of a local defense force being an American or international program does not mean withholding NATO government participation. Instead, the international footprint should be minimal. NATO forces can take several specific actions to minimize public exposure. One is to work with ANA and ANP forces to pro-

---

3 On declining perceptions of the United States see, for example, ABC, BBC, and ARD, "Afghanistan: Where Things Stand," poll, 2009.

4 Jihadist website, February 4, 2009.

vide basic training and guidance to a local defense force (a train-the-trainer program). Determining what training is necessary will require case-by-case evaluations of the competence of local security forces, the threat level in the area, and the competence of ANA and ANP forces conducting training. To facilitate these activities, it would be ideal for NATO forces to live in—or around—the villages in which local defense programs are established to help monitor them and ensure they are not used for offensive purposes or come under the control of warlords or the Taliban. Given their doctrine and historic mission, U.S. SOF are ideally suited for implementing this type of program, which has similarities to the Robin Sage training exercise conducted at the John F. Kennedy Special Warfare Center at Fort Bragg, North Carolina. However, foreign involvement must be temporary. The objective of this program must be an eventual transition to full Afghan control.

In addition, Afghan and NATO forces must demonstrate the will and ability to drive out guerrillas.[5] It might be counterproductive to set up a local defense force when Taliban guerrillas remain poised on the outskirts of the village, ready to strike in retaliation. The local force should be part of the "hold" and "build" part of a "shape, clear, hold, and build" counterinsurgency strategy. Military forces cannot stay in cleared areas indefinitely, and there have also been too few ANA and ANP forces to establish security in rural villages.

Grassroots Initiatives

Local defense forces should originate from the bottom up, not the top down. Indeed, local forces will only be effective if they are grassroots

---

[5] For example, in South Vietnam's Civil Operations and Revolutionary Development Program (CORDS), the first step in that multifaceted counterinsurgency program, successful in many localities, was to expel or destroy any sizeable enemy units. See Stuart E. Methven, *Parapolitics and Pacification: A Study in Applied Cadre Techniques*, Cambridge, Mass.: Massachusetts Institute of Technology, Center for International Studies, 1967, p. 58; David L. Philips, White Paper Proposal Developed for Special Forces: Rural Development Team Project, McLean, Va.: Courage Services, 2009; Austin Long, *On "Other War": Lessons from Five Decades of RAND Corporation Counterinsurgency Research*, Santa Monica, Calif.: RAND Corporation, MG-482-OSD, 2006.

initiatives established to serve local interests. Afghan and NATO forces should look for two types of opportunities. In the first type, tribes, subtribes, clans, villages, or other local institutions have *already* fought or otherwise resisted insurgents. In the second type, local communities have come to Afghan or NATO governments asking for assistance against insurgents. Assessing both types of opportunities requires carefully collecting and analyzing intelligence.

Fortunately, there are numerous examples of grassroots initiatives in which local tribes and communities have resisted insurgents or asked Afghan or NATO forces for assistance. Examples include Noorzais, Barakzais, Achokzais, and Alikozais in the west and south and Shinwaris, Kharotis, Mangals, Chamkanis, Moqbils, Zadrans, and Jajis in the east.[6] The Village Stability Platform, a joint Afghan-ISAF effort to engage villages, was established in 2009 as a bottom-up strategy to provide local security, enable development, and foster Afghan governance. It brought key tribal and other community leaders into the political process and linked villages to district and provincial governments. As part of the Village Stability Platform, Afghan and NATO officials identified a series of grassroots initiatives.

Locals, including Pashtuns, have offered several reasons for resisting insurgents in response to the following Taliban practices:

- terrorism, including killing of civilians
- taxation of civilians
- demands for fuel, food, and support
- recruitment of young men
- school closures
- bans on music and other traditional cultural manifestations.

In some areas, locals view insurgents as attracting deadly military raids and air strikes. Keeping the Taliban out is seen as a way of also keeping out foreign troops who will break down doors, search homes, and inflict other forms of harm and humiliation. Because the local

---

[6] Author interviews with tribal and other community leaders in eastern, southern, and western Afghanistan, 2009.

communities have lost hope that the ANA or ANP can protect them, they prefer to raise their own village forces. Indeed, the primary areas for leveraging local forces are in the western, southern, and eastern areas most affected by the insurgency—which are nearly all Pashtun.

Bottom-up efforts should primarily focus on Pashtun areas because they represent the key insurgent areas and because they are less likely to be co-opted by warlords. As Antonio Giustozzi argued, warlordism has historically been much less pervasive in Pashtun areas of Afghanistan.[7]

Legitimate Institutions

Local forces, such as arbakai, have generally been most effective when they are established by legitimate local institutions. Jirgas and shuras represent Pashtun versions of democratic institutions because the participants are leaders who represent their tribal and other constituents.[8] In practical terms, the jirga or shura should decide whether it wants a local defense force, choose which individuals should participate in it, oversee what tasks it performs, coordinate with Afghan government officials, and decide when to disband it. A 2008 opinion poll that the Asia Foundation conducted indicated that most Afghans do not trust warlords, and only 4 percent said they would turn to a local warlord to deal with a local security problem.[9] Forces under the control of warlords have generally been unpopular because they are used to benefit individuals, rather than tribes or other local institutions. In addition, local forces have often been most effective when they support local interests, especially defending local villages for the sake of the village, rather than the central government or foreigners.

---

[7] Giustozzi, *Empires of Mud*, p. 36.

[8] In practice, there are often competing jirgas and shuras at the village, district, and provincial levels. Consequently, deciphering which are "legitimate" and which are "illegitimate" can sometimes be difficult for outsiders. In addition, the Taliban have targeted tribal leaders in some areas that resist their activity. Many have been killed, while others have fled to such cities as Kabul and Kandahar.

[9] Asia Foundation, *Afghanistan in 2008*.

Having local shuras and jirgas exercise command and control over local defense forces also means ensuring that central government forces do not attempt to establish formal control. To attract communities to participate, local autonomy should be maintained. As noted earlier, central government forces should retain the preponderance of power and provide oversight, training, and other support. Given historical precedents and local preferences, however, we assess that the Ministry of Interior or other Afghan ministries, such as the Ministry of Defense, should not exert direct command and control over local forces. The central government established overt command and control for the Afghan Public Protection Program in Wardak Province, as shown in Figure 5.1, where local Afghan protectors reported directly to the ANP district police chief. As one study warned:

> [T]he Afghan government lacks capacity to even monitor its own security forces, let alone community-based policing structures. A

Figure 5.1
Afghan Public Protection Force Command and Control

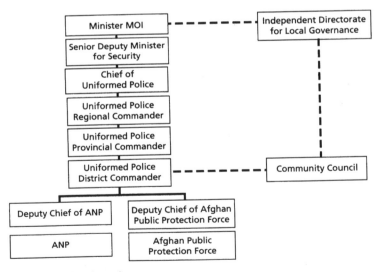

SOURCE: Author interviews.
RAND MG1002-5.1

better approach might be for the state to function as a facilitator, as it did successfully during the presidential and parliamentary elections (with Chief of Police and Provincial Governor working with a multi-community shura). This would mean that arbakai retain their autonomy and community linkages, but still have some form of limited oversight—which is often readily desired by local communities.[10]

An unclassified draft Afghan-NATO proposal in early 2010 defined local defense forces participating in the Village Stability Platform as auxiliary forces of the district police chief. The ANP would exercise command and control over these units, including approving their size. The Ministry of Interior would pay these forces, which would have to submit to a lengthy list of requirements, including biometric screening and a loyalty oath. According to this proposal, the Afghan government would only establish local forces in villages where there was no poppy cultivation and no "narcotics consumption"—an unnecessary and unrealistic caveat. Some elements of the plan were laudable, such as limiting patrols to village boundaries. However, the proposal was a clear central government effort to control local defense forces. Local jirgas and shuras are bound to oppose direct government control, even though they may be willing to collaborate with the government.

The shura or jirga should manage the local defense force, including selecting the members and setting the terms for their participation. We suggest that rotation be considered. To prevent creating a permanent body of armed men, different members of the community should be tasked to participate at different times over the course of a year. Ideally, the dangers and benefits of local defense force membership should be spread as widely as possible throughout the community. The jirga or shura should control funding to cover local defense force operating expenses. In sum, this option entails empowering the jirga or shura, not the local defense force itself.[11]

---

[10] Schmeidl and Karokhail, "The Role of Non-State Actors," p. 334.

[11] Author interviews with Pashtun tribal leader, Afghanistan, May 2009.

Quick-Reaction Capability

Between 2007 and 2010, the most demoralizing aspect of the Pakistan effort to use lashkars against local militants was the government's inability to protect the tribesmen from retaliation. Similar events have happened in Afghanistan as well. It would be counterproductive to have local communities stand up to the Taliban and then be overrun. Consequently, an essential part of any local defense program should be establishing a quick-response force that is on standby 24 hours a day to come to the assistance of the local defense force. This quick-response force could incorporate both Afghan and NATO units. Providing security to the local population should be the top priority of NATO forces, as opposed to chasing the enemy and killing enemy combatants.[12]

A corollary to the quick-response force is a communication system that connects villages to the quick-response force to ensure timely receipt of any call for help. Communication between a local defense force and the quick-response force should not only be about force protection but also about general intelligence on enemy movements in the area and on their activities and capabilities. The specific type of communication equipment is beyond the scope of this document. Some of the issues that need to be addressed include whether to provide encrypted radios (in addition to cell phones and satellite phones), what type of antenna to use, where to locate the equipment, and who will be responsible for it. One or more of these communication systems may fall into the hands of the enemy, and this technical assistance should be handled accordingly.

Development Programs

A key facet of a local defense forces plan should be to bring jobs, schools, health clinics, and other improvements to participating communities. Coordination with the Independent Directorate of Local Governance,

---

[12] See, for example, David Kilcullen, *The Accidental Guerrilla*, New York: Oxford University Press, 2009.

Ministry of Rural Rehabilitation and Development, U.S. Agency for International Development, and other Afghan and international development agencies would also be important to facilitate the implementation of projects and to provide incentives for communities establishing local defense forces. The program should offer not only improved security to participating communities but also tangible development benefits.

As noted previously, Afghan and NATO forces should not, if possible, pay local defense members because individuals should be motivated to work for their communities and not for outsiders. Some local leaders emphatically told us that paying salaries for what should be community service would attract the wrong kinds of recruits. If the Taliban were to offer more money, such recruits would easily switch sides. In addition, paying salaries adds logistical problems. In 2005 and 2006, for example, Afghan government efforts to pay local arbakai in Paktia Province ran into problems when funding dried up.[13] A better approach may be to provide development aid that benefits the communities. As one study concludes,

> [p]utting community leaders on government pay roll does not only strip them of their autonomy, but can also lead to corruption if there is no accountability on how they in turn pay the arbakai guards. A better alternative might be to find ways to support entire communities in return for the contributing to security. Then it becomes a mutually beneficial relationship rather than a one-way dependency.[14]

Indeed, a rising complaint against the Afghan government is that it has not provided basic services to the population, especially in rural areas.[15] For maximum psychological effect, tribal elders should be asked what projects their communities need, rather than have outside development experts make that determination. Afghanistan's Min-

---

[13] Ruttig, "Loya Paktia's Insurgency," pp. 68–69, 86.

[14] Schmeidl and Karokhail, "The Role of Non-State Actors," p. 333.

[15] See, for example, Seth G. Jones, *In the Graveyard of Empires: America's War in Afghanistan*, New York: W.W. Norton, 2009.

istry of Rural Rehabilitation and Development has tried to do this with its community development councils, which were established to help communities oversee development projects in their areas. Public opinion surveys should also be conducted wherever possible. The U.S. Agency for International Development has implemented a framework to identify, prioritize, and mitigate the causes of instability—and to serve as a baseline for development aid—called the Tactical Conflict Assessment and Planning Framework. It includes a list of questions to ask villagers, such as the following: Have there been changes in the village population in the last year? What are the most important problems facing the village? Who do you believe can solve your problems? What should be done first to help the village?[16]

The Taliban and other insurgents understand the use of development projects for counterinsurgency and have attacked projects designed to win hearts and minds. Insurgents have threatened, killed, or kidnapped foreign and Afghan aid workers and sabotaged infrastructure. Any effort to gain arbakai collaboration by favoring their communities with special assistance would likely draw a violent reaction from insurgents. Therefore, the quick-response force should not only protect a local defense force in the face of expected insurgent attacks but perhaps also take on the civic action projects that the insurgents would likely seek to destroy.

Psychological and Information Operations

Some of the most serious obstacles to implementing an effective counterinsurgency campaign in Afghanistan are psychological. The Afghan and U.S. governments are not popular in some areas of Afghanistan, and many consider U.S. military forces to be a foreign army of occupation. Taliban propaganda skillfully exploits these negative views and focuses on the civilian casualties that U.S. and NATO military strikes have caused. Effective counterpropaganda is essential

---

[16] U.S. Agency for International Development, *Tactical Conflict Assessment and Planning Framework*, Kabul, 2009.

to counterinsurgency success. This means addressing target audiences in a manner that conforms to their attitudes and perceptions, using media that are accessible to them and that are credible, and relying on influential key communicators. The Taliban and other groups have exploitable vulnerabilities. They have created significant resentment because of terrorist acts that kill innocent civilians, public beheadings, targeted assassinations, sabotage of girls' schools, and other actions. The Taliban call for jihad presents the conflict as one between Islam and infidels (and their local lackeys). A local defense program can fundamentally change the discourse—and reality—to one between local Afghans and fanatics trying to impose an extremist ideology. To regain the initiative, Afghan and NATO forces should focus on local grievances, developing a counterpropaganda program closely attuned to the aspirations of the communities in which the local defense force would operate.

Members of the local defense force and their communities can serve as a focus group to sound out the viability of proposed themes and messages. We suggest expanding the standard use of a focus group and involving locals in developing, not just evaluating, messages. This would not necessarily entail direct contact between U.S. military information and psychological operations personnel, which could tag the locals as foreign collaborators. But the interaction could be done through Afghan intermediaries who have agreed to cooperate, both in and out of government circles. Such operational details would vary from place to place, depending on the particular situation. The general principle is to use the local defense force program as a means of gaining local participation in a propaganda campaign to discredit the Taliban and improve the image of the Afghan government and security forces.

In a largely illiterate society for which verbal, face-to-face communication is the most important way to send and receive information, the jirgas and local defense forces could also become conduits for message dissemination. The same mechanism could be used for measuring the effectiveness of information and psychological operations to gauge the effects of Afghan and U.S. information campaigns. Finally, the creation of a local defense force willing to stand up to the Taliban is by itself an excellent psychological operation. If a significant number of Pashtun communities could be persuaded to take this step, the collective result would be a major psychological and political blow to the insurgency.

Intelligence

Traditionally, a common aspect of the arbakai system is the *kishakee* collectors of information. Their job is to spy on the enemy and gather information on its whereabouts, armed capabilities, and (if possible) intentions. Through their own network of informants the *kishakee* endeavor to keep the jirgas and the arbakai apprised of threats to the community.[17] Government forces setting up arbakai for counterinsurgency purposes would benefit greatly by tapping into this ready-made intelligence gathering network.

In addition, the relatives and friends of a local defense force will now be on the government side and in need of protection from insurgent reprisals. Part of any civilian defense program should be identification, training, and supporting of those most willing and capable of acquiring relevant information. Their goal would be not only to collect intelligence on the Taliban but also information on the local political and economic issues constituting the rich contextual understanding that is essential for good counterinsurgency planning.

Rich cultural understanding, which can also be called *human terrain mapping* or *cultural intelligence*, is essential for setting up viable local defense forces. The following list of suggested questions would help determine the viability of establishing a local defense force:

- *Tribal councils.* Is the traditional tribal structure functioning or not? Does a traditional jirga or shura exist? How much power and influence does it have? How often does it meet? Who are its members? What are their backgrounds? What is their reputation among the people? What tribes, clans, or families do they represent? What major decisions have they made? What issues are they

---

17 Tariq, *Tribal Security System*, pp. 2–3, 7.

dealing with now? What are the internal factions within this jirga or shura? What attitudes does the jirga or shura have toward the government of Afghanistan, the United States, and insurgents?

- *Community defense.* Does an arbakai or something similar already exist? Is there a tradition of arbakai, even if none currently exists? If there is an arbakai, who belongs to it, and to whom do they answer? What is the community's attitude toward this arbakai? What is its record? Whom or what are they guarding against? What is its armed strength? In areas with no functioning tribal institution, is there any kind of nontribal militia or community defense group? If so, who organized it, and who maintains it? Has any local security force expressed a willingness to confront insurgents?

- *Community leadership.* Outside the jirga or shura, who are the key community leaders, within or outside the tribal system? Do warlords exist in the area who have the power to impose themselves on the community and shape events? Who are the main drug traffickers or other powerful criminal elements? Who are the most influential mullahs or other religious figures? What are their backgrounds? What do they preach? How powerful are they in shaping community decisions? Who are the key communicators outside the religious sphere?[18]

- *Tribal mapping.* What are the major tribes, subtribes, and clans in the locality, and what specific communities do they occupy? Which tribes, subtribes, and clans are allies or friendly with each other, and which are enemies? Are there specific reasons for the hostilities? What are the attitudes of the different tribal groupings toward the government of Afghanistan, the United States, and insurgents? Which communities favor the insurgents, and which do not?[19]

---

[18] These individuals may vary greatly from place to place and may not be part of the traditional tribal system. They may be wealthy merchants, schoolteachers, medical doctors, government officials, and others. Getting them to support a local defense force could be crucial.

[19] The latter might be a good starting point for creating a local defense force.

- *Insurgency.* What is the relationship between insurgents and the tribes in each locality? Do most insurgents come from there? Are local insurgent commanders natives of the areas in which they operate, or are they outsiders? What points are salient in the interaction between insurgents and local communities? Are insurgents trying to win over the people primarily by persuasion or intimidation? Have they kidnapped or killed government supporters and accused informants? Have they attacked nongovernmental organizations or Afghan government personnel implementing development projects? Do the insurgents control certain areas? What is the extent of their "shadow government"? How aggressive are the insurgents in terms of attacking Afghan or NATO forces? How likely is an attack against a local defense force?
- *Economy.* What are the major economic activities in a given locality? What is the main means of livelihood? What are the main economic interest groups? Who are the economic elites? Are there economic factors in tribal rivalries? Is there an economic disparity between those who support insurgents and those who do not? Would a local defense force be associated with a particular economic group? How important is poppy cultivation to the locals?
- *Grievances.* What are the population's major complaints? Are the grievances based on economics, security, education, governance, corruption, land or water disputes, tribal, divisions, or other factors?[20]

Tribal and community engagement will almost inevitably require reintegrating middle- and lower-level Taliban and other insurgents. Reintegrating insurgents can be an extremely delicate endeavor. A number of tribal leaders in the south, for example, have cooperated with the Taliban and with Afghan and NATO forces, depending on their shifting self-interests and assessment of which side is winning.

Several issues need to be addressed in weighing the costs and benefits of reintegration. First, are reintegration candidates currently on a

---

[20] The inquiry into grievances should also explore attitudes toward the Afghan and U.S. governments, with specific examples of past experiences, both positive and negative.

targeting list or the United Nations Security Council blacklist?[21] Negotiating with insurgents on these lists would require the approval and involvement of the highest levels of the Afghan government. Second, can they be trusted? Gaining fidelity on this question will likely necessitate interaction with individuals, careful information collection and analysis, and perhaps some preliminary tests to gauge the seriousness of their intentions. Third, how malign is the individual? In some cases, it may not be politically feasible to reconcile someone who has significant American or Afghan blood on his hands or is a major drug trafficker.

Regarding this process, there has been a long-standing debate on amnesty for Taliban insurgents. Amnesty requires a formal agreement not to prosecute the individual in question for crimes committed while an insurgent. However, there are no guidelines as to how that would be achieved. Presidential pardon would be the easiest mechanism, but that would require the Afghan president to sign off on every application. With higher-level commanders who might be on a United Nations or U.S. blacklist, the concern is not only amnesty but also power sharing. Accustomed to being commanders, these individuals will not easily go back to farming or other menial jobs. They want positions in the Afghan government and the right to participate in national and local politics. If Taliban commanders do receive such concessions as the price of their defection from the insurgency, it would enhance the cause of peace in southern and eastern Afghanistan. But it might lead to violent protests in the north and center, where the Tajiks and Hazaras suffered atrocities at the hands of the Taliban.

---

[21] United Nations Security Council, Resolution 1267, New York, October 15, 1999. The committee established under this resolution created and maintains the Consolidated List "with respect to Al-Qaida, Usama bin Laden, and the Taliban and other individuals, groups, undertakings and entities associated with them." We used the January 25, 2010, update.

CHAPTER SIX

Mitigating Risks

Effectively leveraging local communities should significantly improve counterinsurgency prospects. First, it can facilitate mobilization of the population against insurgents, as has already occurred in parts of southern Afghanistan through the Village Stability Platform. The support of the population is the sine qua non of victory in counterinsurgency warfare, especially mobilizing locals to fight insurgents, provide information on their location and movement, and deny insurgent sanctuary in their areas.[1] As Stathis Kalyvas concludes in his wide-ranging study of insurgencies, the formation of local self-defense programs "is an essential part of counterinsurgency efforts" to organize communities. While the

> members may be focused on defending their villages or families, the fact that they are permanently present in their villages and are operating in places they know well allows incumbents to tap into private information.[2]

---

[1] Trinquier, *Modern Warfare*, p. 6.

[2] Stathis N. Kalyvas, *The Logic of Violence in Civil War*, New York: Cambridge University Press, 2006, p. 107. Also see, for example, Christian Geffray, *La Cause des Armes au Mozambique: Anthropologie d'une Guerre Civile*, Paris: Éditions Karthala, 1990; Richard Stubbs, *Hearts and Minds in Guerrilla Warfare: The Malayan Emergency, 1948–1960*, New York: Oxford University Press, 1989; Marie-Joelle Zahar, "Proteges, Clients, Cannon Fodder: Civil-Militia Relations in Internal Conflicts," in Simon Chesterman, ed., *Civilians in War*, Boulder, Colo.: Lynne Riener, 2001.

Villagers have a much better understanding of the terrain and local networks, including the location and movement of insurgents. "To carry out a war effectively, to win it," wrote the French counterinsurgency soldier and author Roger Trinquier, "it is indispensable to identify the adversary exactly."[3]

By tapping into tribes and other communities where there is *already* grassroots resistance, local defense forces can help mobilize communities simultaneously across multiple areas, as the British effectively did in Malaya using indigenous self-defense organizations.[4] The goal should be to help cause a "cascade" or "tip," in which momentum against the Taliban becomes unstoppable.[5] Social scientists have explored the phenomena of cascades and tips for riots, revolutions, and other events. Cascades often occur because people's choices about their actions are based on what they think others are likely to do.[6] One of the best examples of the tipping model is the fall of the Taliban regime in 2001. The mobilization of Tajiks, Uzbeks, Hazaras, and ultimately Pashtun communities in November 2001 caused a tip in the war as momentum against the Taliban became too strong to overcome. Barely a month after the bombing campaign started, a series of cities fell to U.S. and Afghan forces—such as Mazar-e-Sharif on November 10, Taloqan and Bamiyan on November 11, and Herat on November 11— until Kabul fell on November 13. The mobilization of local communities was critical to establishing momentum against the Taliban.[7]

Second, working with communities counters the Taliban's primary advantage: their largely unchallenged ability to co-opt or coerce

---

3   Trinquier, *Modern Warfare*, p. 23.

4   Hughes and Tripodi, "Anatomy of a Surrogate."

5   Thomas Schelling, *Micromotives and Macrobehavior*, New York: Norton, 1978; Timur Kuran, "New Out of Never: The Role of Surprise in the East European Revolution of 1989," *World Politics*, Vol. 44, No. 1, 1991.

6   David D. Laitin, *Identity in Formation: The Russian-Speaking Populations in the Near Abroad*, Ithaca, N.Y.: Cornell University Press, 1998, pp. 21–24.

7   See, for example, Stephen Biddle, *Afghanistan and the Future of Warfare: Implications for Army and Defense Policy*, Carlisle, Penn.: Strategic Studies Institute, U.S. Army War College, November 2002.

local communities. Since December 2001, there has been little effort to counter the Taliban and other insurgent groups at the local level by co-opting tribes, subtribes, clans, *qawms*, and other communities. For instance, after the October 2007 death of Alikozai leader Mullah Naqib in Arghandab, a strategically important district north of Kandahar City, the Taliban orchestrated an effective effort to coerce and co-opt Alikozais. They took advantage of grievances when President Karzai, a Popalzai, chose Mullah Nequib's 26-year-old son as the new Alikozai leader, an appointment that is traditionally made by the tribe. The Taliban quickly surged into Arghandab and neighboring districts, including Khakrez. The Afghan government and NATO made little effort to counter the Taliban among Alikozais, leaving control of Arghandab and several of the surrounding districts to the Taliban by 2009.[8] This was unfortunate since the Alikozais were strongly anti-Taliban prior to Mullah Naqib's death.

Third, establishing local defense forces can improve the central government's relationship with local communities by bringing the two together—especially in rural areas where there is little or no government presence. The involvement of provincial governors, district governors, police, and army forces in providing oversight and mentoring to local communities can strengthen central government ties to the periphery, as it did during the Musahiban dynasty. Key mechanisms to improve ties include the establishment of a quick-response force tied to Afghan national security forces; a communication system that allows local and national forces to share information; a development program through such organizations as the Ministry of Rural Rehabilitation and Development; and vetting, training, and mentoring by Afghan national forces.

Yet local defense forces must be part of a broader counterinsurgency strategy. We have focused on security measures, but effective counterinsurgency requires progress on multiple fronts: raising the competence of national security forces, improving governance (including combating corruption), reintegrating insurgents, and improving

---

[8] Carl Forsberg, *The Taliban's Campaign in Kandahar*, Washington, D.C.: The Institute for the Study of War, 2009, pp. 37–41.

economic and other development conditions. As the Nobel Prize-winning economist Amartya Sen argued,

> [p]olitical freedoms (in the form of free speech and elections) help to promote economic security. Social opportunities (in the form of education and health facilities) facilitate economic participation. Economic facilities (in the form of opportunities for participation in trade and production) can help to generate personal abundance as well as public resources for social facilities.[9]

In addition to understanding the potential benefits of a local defense program, the concerns critics have voiced should also be addressed. One is that local defense forces in Afghanistan have a history of failure and are inherently unreliable. When the government sends the arbakai on campaigns outside their communities, the chances for abuses or mistakes increase. When the arbakai stick to patrolling their own communities, they have a good track record. Those who argue civilian defense forces have always played a negative role ignore that record.

In addition, some have argued that the United States has tried this before and that it did not work, referring to the now-terminated Afghan National Auxiliary Police program. This argument is flawed because the Afghan National Auxiliary Police were not based on arbakai or other traditional policing institutions. Moreover, critics often argue that local defense forces should not be used as a substitute for the Afghan army and police. We agree. They should not be used as a substitute for national forces but rather as a supplement, as they have historically been used. Expansion of the Afghan army and police are critical to counterinsurgency success. A key role of local defense forces is to free troops that would otherwise be tied down to patrolling villages and providing local security, so that they can be used to conduct offensive operations against insurgents.

Additional concerns are that civilian defense forces will

- increase violence in the countryside
- strengthen warlords

---

9   Amartya Sen, *Development as Freedom*, New York: Anchor Books, 2000, p. 11.

- weaken central government forces
- undermine efforts to disarm and demobilize armed groups in Afghanistan, especially disarmament, demobilization, and reintegration (DDR) and disbandment of illegally armed groups (DIAG) programs
- use the program for political purposes, such as rewarding tribes close to senior government officials.

The following sections address each of these concerns in turn.

Violence in the Countryside

Rural communities in Afghanistan often maintain intense rivalries with each other because of factors ranging from land boundaries and water rights to *badal* (revenge for violated honor). Some might fear that local defense forces in this environment would inevitably turn on each other. This argument posits that the Afghan government and NATO may achieve the short-term goal of constraining insurgent activity but make things worse over the long run by increasing the likelihood of inter- and intratribal warfare. There is always a possibility that villages and tribes will fight each other, and some blood feuds have lasted hundreds of years.

This concern seems to have been substantiated recently in the case of the Shinwari elders who offered to wage their own campaign against the Taliban at a January 2010 meeting in Jalalabad with U.S. military officers. Eager to encourage this type of tribal initiative against the insurgency, the Americans responded with an offer to fund development projects. Unfortunately, instead of fighting the Taliban, the Shinwari began attacking each other in March. A land dispute between two subtribes erupted in violence, killing 13 people.

To prevent such a violent outbreak from vitiating a local defense program, several control mechanisms should be implemented. First, an effective local defense program presupposes a permanent relationship with the Afghan army in which the latter will monitor the local patrols, provide training and support, ensure they stay within the parameters of the program, and serve as the immediate reaction force. At present, in the Village Stability Platform, NATO and Afghan National Security Forces are performing these functions. However, the presence of these teams is temporary. The long-term strategy must be to ensure that Afghan national forces increasingly run the program.

Another control mechanism is the provision of benefits. In the current Village Stability Platform, the U.S. SOF teams reside in the villages; work closely with the local jirgas and shuras; and help coordinate development projects, schools, health clinics, and other types of aid. Preliminary reports from Village Stability Platform villages indicate considerable success in this endeavor. Development projects in one Kandahar community have created 500 new jobs. A refurbished school is attracting students from neighboring villages because parents consider it safe to send their children there. However, these benefits are contingent on avoiding internecine strife. The basic appeal is to self-interest. Villagers will most likely think twice about jeopardizing gains in health care, education, and jobs by reverting to traditional feuding.

Finally, there has been too much emphasis on the vengeance aspect of the *Pashtunwali* and not enough on the mechanisms in the same code of tribal law facilitating negotiation between enemies and conflict resolution.[10] Most importantly, in terms of mediation of conflict, there is a role for the central government. During the Musahibin Dynasty, the Afghan kings played this role. In the case of the land dispute among the Shinwaris, one of the tribal elders complained publicly that the government should have stepped in to mediate. A local defense program should facilitate this type of mediating role for the central government by creating a relationship of trust and cooperation. Thus, the type of program envisioned should actually help diminish rural violence rather than increase it.

---

[10] Barfield, "Culture and Custom." Also see, for example, Barth, "Pathan Identity and Its Maintenance."

Warlord Militias

Some might argue that local forces will promote a return to warlordism. The indiscriminate use of the term *militia* confuses the issue. There is a profound difference between warlord General Abdul Rashid Dostum's militia, comprising thousands of combatants with tanks and heavy weapons, and the traditional Pashtun village policing forces that are the subject of this assessment. As Antonio Giustozzi argues in his study of warlords in Afghanistan, a warlord is a "charismatic and patrimonial military leader with autonomous control over a military force capable of achieving/maintaining a monopoly of large scale violence over a sizeable territory."[11] A critical component of a warlord is the personal nature of his power, which is used to strengthen an individual, not a community. As Giustozzi points out, warlord militias have been most prevalent in Tajik and Uzbek areas of northern and western Afghanistan. These warlord militias are culturally distinct from traditional policing institutions, such as arbakai, chagha, and chalweshtai. The fundamental difference is that the traditional system is based on the collective authority of the jirga, whereas modern warlord militias are based on an individual who places himself above the tribe. The two systems are fundamentally opposed to each other. It is a mistake to equate the two.

The first step toward impeding the resurgence of warlords and their militias is to work through legitimate local institutions, not individuals. Arbakai have traditionally been established through local jirgas and shuras, rather than warlords. As one study concludes, many policymakers with a superficial understanding of Afghan traditions tend to "lump militia of all kinds into the same category as customary structures such as the arbakai (community-based policing) or the lashkar (tribal army)."[12] Furthermore, through human terrain mapping and the rich contextual understanding of the operating environment, Afghan and NATO forces need to identify which leaders are warlords who are primarily interested in increasing their own power bases, not

---

[11] Giustozzi, *Empires of Mud*, p. 5.

[12] Schmeidl and Karokhail, "The Role of Non-State Actors," p. 319.

in supporting their communities. Another measure that should be taken to impede the rise of warlord militias is to be sure that local defense forces remain small, village level, defensive, and focused on patrolling the communities in which their members reside. In addition, it may make sense for Afghan and NATO forces to live in—or near—communities in which local defense forces are established to provide oversight and to ensure they remain small and defensive. Finally, as noted previously, NATO should continue building competent Afghan national army and police forces, which retain a preponderance of power. One of the most significant causes of warlordism during the 1990s was the collapse of the Afghan government and the disbanding of a national army.

The National Army and Police

Some might be concerned that local defense forces will undermine central government security institutions, especially the ANA and ANP. The concern is that empowering local leaders may help the Afghan government and the United States achieve short-term goals but will undermine stability over the long run by fragmenting authority. This is an academic debate. Social and cultural realities make it impossible to neglect local leaders because they hold much of the power today. Indeed, this risk can be mitigated in several ways.

First, Afghan national security institutions should be deeply interlinked with local forces through vetting, training, mentoring, establishing a quick-response force to respond to insurgent attacks, and playing arbitrator among tribes, subtribes, clans, and *qawms* when there is conflict. As already noted, a successful local defense program should improve the connection between the central government and local institutions. Second, central government security forces have rarely established law and order in rural Afghanistan through a permanent presence. Expecting the central government to do this today fails to take into account Afghan history and culture. Instead, order has historically been established through a confluence of top-down efforts of the central government (especially in urban areas) and bottom-up efforts of local actors (especially in rural areas). Third, there are not enough Coalition or Afghan national security forces to provide security in rural areas of Afghanistan, and there will not be enough for the foreseeable future. Consequently, it is hard to see how creating a local defense force would weaken what does not exist. If there were enough soldiers and police to counter the insurgency, the local force might be an impediment. But the numbers of soldiers and police are far below those needed.

Demobilization and Disarmament Efforts

Some might argue that establishing local defense forces will undermine efforts to implement DDR of excombatants, as well as the DIAG program. But this argument fails to understand the most serious problem with Afghan disarmament programs: It is nearly impossible to disarm groups in the midst of a war. Most successful disarmament programs in such countries as Mozambique, El Salvador, and Namibia took place after the war ended.[13] Expecting disarmament to work in the midst of an insurgency is wishful thinking, especially given Afghanistan's history. The inherent problem with DDR and DIAG since 2001 is that war provides an incentive for locals to keep their weapons to protect themselves. In addition, the disarmament of local forces has been uneven and biased. One result of the DDR and DIAG programs was a vacuum in the countryside, which Taliban guerrillas and bandits proceeded to fill. Even more problematic, the Taliban recruited demobilized and jobless personnel into their ranks who had been through the DDR and DIAG programs.[14]

Nonetheless, a local defense program should include a demobilization component to be instituted when the security situation improves.

---

[13] Colin Gleichman, Michael Odenwald, Kees Steenken, and Adrian Wilkinson, *Disarmament, Demobilization and Reintegration: A Practical Field and Classroom Guide*, Frankfurt, Germany: Druckerei Hassmuller Graphische Betriebe, 2004; Eric Berman, *Managing Arms in Peace Processes: Mozambique, Disarmament and Conflict Resolution Project*, United Nations Institute for Disarmament Research, Geneva: United Nations Publications, 1996.

[14] Elias, "The Resurgence of the Taliban in Kabul," p. 53.

This might include at least two types of demobilization. The first is demobilization through traditional tribal methods. Tribal defense forces, such as arbakai, are temporary. Arbakai have generally been called when there is a threat to the community, and the size and scope of local defense forces should decrease as the threat subsides.[15] Consequently, successful efforts to secure an area should cause the local jirga or shura to demobilize local defense force members over time, although it may be necessary to keep a small force in place to protect against criminal groups.

Ideally, local defense forces should not experience the same problems as demobilizing guerrillas or regular military forces because they have a limited role to protect their own communities. The optimal situation would entail using part-time members on rotation so that they can continue their normal economic activities while serving in the local defense force. In addition, it may be a good idea to avoid creating a cadre of armed men in the community who enjoy special status and begin seeing armed patrols as their main livelihood. The practical reality, however, is that, in some locations, it may be necessary to field full-time local defense forces that receive salaries. The traditional tribal system does not function in all areas, and it may be naïve to assume that volunteers will perform unpaid community service in all cases. Even in traditional tribal areas, the pressures of unemployment and poverty may lead local jirgas to pay the arbakai, chalweshtai, or other local forces. Nontribal local defense forces may expect to be paid. In these cases, it may be appropriate to develop a more-formal DDR program.

Under most disarmament programs, combatants hand over weapons to international or local authorities, who are responsible for their collection, safe storage, disposal, or destruction. In Afghanistan, handing weapons to foreign troops will be difficult. In the case of local defense forces, which patrol with their own weapons, expecting them to turn weapons over to the government at the end of the program may be seen as betrayal. Demobilization usually entails registering,

---

[15] See, for example, Richard F. Strand, "The Evolution of Anti-Communist Resistance in Eastern Nuristan," in Shahrani and Canfield, eds., *Revolutions and Rebellions*, p. 91.

counting, and monitoring combatants, then preparing them for discharge. Reintegration is the process under which combatants reenter the civilian work force. The objective of reintegration programs is to assist former combatants in socially and economically reintegrating into civilian society so that they do not turn to banditry or violence.

Government Manipulation of Tribes and Other Communities for Political Purposes

Some might be concerned that the government will create local defense forces for political purposes. The concern that the Afghan government will try to manipulate tribal politics is not limited to local defense forces but extends to many aspects of governance, from elections to political appointments. For centuries, Afghan officials have tried to manipulate tribes, subtribes, clans, *qawms*, and other communities for political purposes—such as targeting enemies and acquiring political support. As one Pashtun axiom notes: "Me against my brothers; me and my brothers against our cousins; me, my brothers, and my cousins against everyone." While Taliban leaders have tried to manipulate tribes, so has the current Afghan government. The 2009 presidential elections were marred by substantial fraud, in which nearly 1 million votes for President Hamid Karzai were thrown out because of fraud, as were another 100,000 for Abdullah Abdullah. For local defense forces, the most significant danger is that government officials could use them as a tool to strengthen some tribes. As already noted, the government has tended to support a few tribes in the south, such as Popalzais and Barakzais, at the expense of others.

Preventing the misuse of local defense forces requires several mitigating steps. First is close coordination between the Afghan government and NATO on the locations of local defense programs, including strict criteria for selecting areas (such as the existence of grassroots initiatives). Second, and most important, local defense programs need to be established with a range of tribes and communities. The existence of local resistance to the Taliban in the west (such as Tajiks and Noorzais), south (such as Alikozais, Noorzais, Achakzais, and Hazaras), east (such as Mangals, Moqbils, Zadrans, and Kharotis), and other areas makes this feasible. However, Afghan and NATO officials will need to monitor developments carefully, making it important to use Afghan and NATO forces in the field for mentoring and oversight.

Conclusions

Top-down efforts to establish security through the central government are likely to fail unless they include a more-effective bottom-up strategy that leverages local communities, especially in rural areas. As one study concludes, "the recent history of Afghanistan is one of revolts against the central power and of resistance to the penetration of the countryside by state bureaucracy."[16]

An effective counterinsurgency strategy that secures the local population needs to focus on improving the competence of central government institutions, including the army and police. But it also needs to leverage bottom-up initiatives where tribes and other local communities have resisted the Taliban. Former U.S. Speaker of the House of Representatives Tip O'Neill could have been talking about Afghanistan when he quipped that "all politics is local." Establishing local defense forces where there is a local initiative should be encouraged. But such forces also need to be carefully managed by the Afghan government, with support from NATO forces. "We need to subcontract security in some areas to local villagers," Minister of Interior Mohammad Hanif Atmar remarked. "And then let Afghan and coalition forces target insurgents in between."[17] In short, villages that establish local defense forces would provide self-defense in their villages—and only in their villages—and ANA, ANP, and NATO forces could conduct offensive operations outside of villages.

Carefully implemented and managed, the Village Stability Platform should be able to minimize the risks and maximize the benefits of leveraging local security forces. Keeping forces small, defensive, under

---

16 Roy, *Islam and Resistance in Afghanistan*, p. 10.

17 Author interview with Minister of Interior Mohammad Hanif Atmar, September 2009.

the direct control of local jirgas and shuras, and monitored by Afghan national and NATO forces should prevent the rise of warlord militias. A number of tribes and local communities have already expressed a desire to stand up to the Taliban and other insurgents. The Afghan government and NATO forces need to take advantage of these opportunities. As one senior Afghan government official recently noted, "It's the only way out of this situation."[18]

---

[18] Author interview with Afghanistan cabinet minister, October 2009.

About the Authors

Seth G. Jones is a senior political scientist at the RAND Corporation and author, most recently, of *In the Graveyard of Empires: America's War in Afghanistan* (W.W. Norton, 2009). In 2009, he served as a plans officer and advisor to the Commanding General, U.S. Special Operations Forces, in Afghanistan. In addition, he has been an adjunct professor in the Security Studies Program at Georgetown University, as well as the Center for Homeland Defense at the U.S. Naval Postgraduate School. He is the author of *The Rise of European Security Cooperation* (Cambridge University Press, 2007). He has also published journal articles on Afghanistan, Pakistan, and other national security subjects in *International Security, Foreign Affairs, The National Interest, Security Studies, Chicago Journal of International Law, International Affairs,* and *Survival,* as well as such newspapers as the *New York Times, Wall Street Journal,* and *Washington Post.* His most recent RAND publications include *Counterinsurgency in Pakistan* (2010), *Counterinsurgency in Afghanistan* (2008), and *How Terrorist Groups End: Lessons for Countering Al Qa'ida* (2008). He received his M.A. and Ph.D. from the University of Chicago.

Arturo Muñoz is a senior political scientist at the RAND Corporation. Prior to joining RAND in February 2009, Muñoz served 29 years at the Central Intelligence Agency, both in the Directorate of Operations and in the Directorate of Intelligence. In his last post, he was a Supervisor/Operations Officer at the CIA Counterterrorism Center. At the CIA, Muñoz created successful counterterrorism, counterinsurgency, and counternarcotics programs, from initial planning to full implementation in the field. As an analyst, he wrote intelligence assessments on insurgent movements in Latin America. At the other end of the spectrum, as a certified case officer overseas, he recruited and handled agents clandestinely, producing disseminated intelligence reports significant to U.S. foreign policy interests. In various supervisory positions, both at headquarters and in the field, he managed innovative covert action campaigns with verifiable impact in Latin America, Southwest Asia, the Balkans, the Middle East, and North Africa. Muñoz received his B.A. in history and Spanish literature from Loyola University; his A.B.D. in anthropology from the University of California, Los Angeles; and his M.A. in anthropology and Ph.D. in history from Stanford University.

References

ABC, BBC, and ARD, "Afghanistan: Where Things Stand," poll, 2009.

————, "Afghanistan: Where Things Stand," poll, January 2010.

Afghanistan Ministry of Defense, *The National Military Strategy*, Kabul, October 2005.

Afghanistan National Security Council, *National Threat Assessment*, Kabul, 2005.

Amnesty International, "Amnesty International Contacts Taliban Spokesperson, Urges Release of Hostages," New York, August 2, 2007.

Asia Foundation, *Afghanistan in 2008: A Survey of the Afghan People*, Kabul, 2008.

————, *Afghanistan in 2009: A Survey of the Afghan People*, Kabul, 2009.

Barfield, Thomas J., "Weak Links on a Rusty Chain: Structural Weaknesses in Afghanistan's Provincial Government Administration," in Shahrani and Canfield, eds., *Revolutions and Rebellions in Afghanistan*, 1984, pp. 170–183.

————, "Problems in Establishing Legitimacy in Afghanistan," *Iranian Studies*, Vol. 37, No. 2, June 2004, pp. 263–293.

————, "Weapons of the Not So Weak in Afghanistan: Pashtun Agrarian Structure and Tribal Organization for Times of War and Peace," paper presented to the Agrarian Studies Colloquium Series, Yale University, February 23, 2007.

————, *Afghanistan: A Cultural and Political History*, Princeton, N.J.: Princeton University Press, 2010, pp. 195–225.

————, "Culture and Custom in Nation-Building: Law in Afghanistan," *Maine Law Review*, Vol. 60, No. 2, Summer 2008, pp. 347–374.

Barth, Fredrik, ed., *Ethnic Groups and Boundaries: The Social Organization of Culture Difference*, Boston: Little, Brown, 1969.

————, "Pathan Identity and Its Maintenance," in Barth, ed., *Ethnic Groups and Boundaries*, 1969.

Bayley, David, *Patterns of Policing*, New Brunswick, N.J.: Rutgers University Press, 1985.

Berman, Eric, *Managing Arms in Peace Processes: Mozambique, Disarmament and Conflict Resolution Project*, United Nations Institute for Disarmament Research, Geneva: United Nations Publications, 1996.

Biddle, Stephen, *Afghanistan and the Future of Warfare: Implications for Army and Defense Policy*, Carlisle, Penn.: Strategic Studies Institute, U.S. Army War College, November 2002.

Bijlert, Martine van, "Unruly Commanders and Violent Power Struggles: Taliban Networks in Uruzgan," in Giustozzi, ed., *Decoding the New Taliban*, pp. 155–178.

Buffaloe, David L., *Conventional Forces in Low-Intensity Conflict: The 82d Airborne in Firebase Shkin*, Arlington, Va.: Association of the United States Army, Landpower Essay 04-2, 2004.

Callwell, C. E., *Small Wars: Their Principles and Practice*, 3rd ed., Lincoln, Neb.: University of Nebraska Press, 1996.

Chesterman, Simon, ed., *Civilians in War*, Boulder, Colo.: Lynne Riener, 2001.

————, *You, the People: The United Nations, Transitional Administration, and Statebuilding*, New York: Oxford University Press, 2004.

Combined Forces Command–Afghanistan and Altai Consulting, *Afghan National Development Poll*, Kabul, 2005.

Crews, Robert D., and Amin Tarzi, eds., *The Taliban and the Crisis of Afghanistan*, Cambridge, Mass.: Harvard University Press, 2008.

Cullather, Nick, "Damming Afghanistan: Modernization in a Buffer State," *The Journal of American History*, Vol. 89, No. 2, September 2002, pp. 25–30.

Dobbins, James, John G. McGinn, Keith Crane, Seth G. Jones, Rollie Lal, Andrew Rathmell, Rachel M. Swanger, and Anga R. Timilsina, *America's Role in Nation-Building: From Germany to Iraq*, Santa Monica, Calif.: RAND Corporation, MR-1753-RC, 2003. As of April 8, 2010:
http://www.rand.org/pubs/monograph_reports/MR1753/

Dobbins, James, Seth G. Jones, Keith Crane, Andrew Rathmell, Brett Steele, Richard Teltschik, and Anga R. Timilsina, *The UN's Role in Nation-Building: From the Congo to Iraq*, Santa Monica, Calif.: RAND Corporation, MG-304-RC, 2005. As of April 8, 2010:
http://www.rand.org/pubs/monographs/MG304/

Doyle, Michael W., and Nicholas Sambanis, *Making War and Building Peace*, Princeton, N.J.: Princeton University Press, 2006.

Dupree, Louis, *Afghanistan*, New York: Oxford University Press, 1997.

Edelstein, David M., "Occupational Hazards: Why Military Occupations Succeed or Fail," *International Security*, Vol. 29, No. 1, Summer 2004, p. 49–91.

Edwards, David B., *Before Taliban: Genealogies of the Afghan Jihad*, Berkeley, Calif.: University of California Press, 2002.

Elias, Mohammad Osman Tariq, "The Resurgence of the Taliban in Kabul: Logar and Wardak," in Giustozzi, ed., *Decoding the New Taliban*, 2009.

Etzioni, Amitai, *From Empire to Community: A New Approach to International Relations*, New York: Palgrave Macmillan, 2004.

———, "A Self-Restrained Approach to Nation-Building by Foreign Powers," *International Affairs*, Vol. 80, No. 1, 2004, pp. 1–17.

Evans, Anne, Nick Manning, Yasin Osmani, Anne Tully, and Andrew Wilder, *A Guide to Government in Afghanistan*, Washington, D.C.: World Bank, 2004.

Faroosh, Syed Miangul, *The Wali of Swat*, Peshawar: Mian Gul Shahzada Mohammed Abdul Haq Jehanzeb, 1983.

Fearon, James D., and David D. Laitin, "Ethnicity, Insurgency, and Civil War," *American Political Science Review*, Vol. 97, No. 1, February 2003, pp. 75–90.

Freeman, Douglas Southall, *Washington*, New York: Simon and Schuster, 1968.

Forsberg, Carl, *The Taliban's Campaign in Kandahar*, Washington, D.C.: The Institute for the Study of War, 2009.

Fortes, Meyer, and Edward Evans-Pritchard, *African Political Systems*, New York: Oxford University Press, 1970.

Fukuyama, Francis, *State-Building: Governance and World Order in the 21st Century*, Ithaca, N.Y.: Cornell University Press, 2004.

Gajewski, Gregory, et al., "How War, a Tribal Social Structure and Donor Efforts Shape Institutional Change in Afghanistan: A Case Study of the Roads Sector," presented at the 2007 Conference of the European Association for Evolutionary Political Economy, Porto, Portugal, November 1–3, 2007.

Galula, David, *Counterinsurgency Warfare: Theory and Practice*, New York: Praeger, [1964] 2006.

Gant, Jim, *One Tribe at a Time*, Los Angeles: Nine Sisters Imports, 2009.

Gauhar, Altaf, *Ayub Khan: Pakistan's First Military Ruler*, Lahore: Sang-e-Meel Publications, 1993.

Geffray, Christian, *La Cause des Armes au Mozambique: Anthropologie d'une Guerre Civile*, Paris: Éditions Karthala, 1990.

Ghani, Ashraf, and Clare Lockhart, *Fixing Failed States: A Framework for Rebuilding a Fractured World*, New York: Oxford University Press, 2008.

Giraldo, Jeanne K., and Harold A. Trinkunas, eds., *Terrorism Financing and State Responses: A Comparative Perspective*, Stanford, Calif.: Stanford University Press, 2007.

Giustozzi, Antonio, ed., *Decoding the New Taliban: Insights from the Afghan Field*, New York: Columbia University Press, 2009.

————, "The Taliban's Marches: Herat, Farah, Baghdis and Ghor," in Giustozzi, ed., *Decoding the New Taliban*, pp. 211–230.

————, *Empires of Mud: Wars and Warlords in Afghanistan*, New York: Columbia University Press, 2009.

Giustozzi, Antonio, and Noor Ullah, *"Tribes" and Warlords in Southern Afghanistan, 1980–2005*, London: Crisis States Research Centre, Working Paper No. 7, September 2006.

Gleichman, Colin, Michael Odenwald, Kees Steenken, and Adrian Wilkinson, *Disarmament, Demobilization and Reintegration: A Practical Field and Classroom Guide*, Frankfurt, Germany: Druckerei Hassmuller Graphische Betriebe, 2004.

Gonzalez, Alberto, "Going Tribal: Notes on Pacification in the 21st Century," *Anthropology Today*, Vol. 25, No. 2, April 2009, pp. 15–19.

Government of Afghanistan, *Security Sector Reform: Disbandment of Illegal Armed Groups Programme (DIAG) and Disarmament, Demobilisation, and Reintegration Programme (DDR)*, Kabul, October 2005.

Grau, Lester W., and Michael A. Gress, *The Soviet-Afghan War: How a Superpower Fought and Lost*, Lawrence, Kan.: University Press of Kansas, 2002.

Harpviken, Kristian Berg, "Transcending Traditionalism: The Emergence of Non-State Military Formations in Afghanistan," *Journal of Peace Research*, Vol. 34, No. 3, August 1997, pp. 271–287.

Headquarters International Security Assistance Force, "ISAF Commander's Counterinsurgency Guidance," Kabul, 2009.

Hosmer, Stephen T., *The Army's Role in Counterinsurgency and Insurgency*, Santa Monica, Calif.: RAND Corporation, R-3947-A, 1990. As of April 8, 2010: http://www.rand.org/pubs/reports/R3947/

Hughes, Geraint, and Christian Tripodi, "Anatomy of a Surrogate: Historical Precedents and Implications for Contemporary Counter-Insurgency and Counter-Terrorism," *Small Wars & Insurgencies*, Vol. 20, No. 1, March 2009, pp. 1–35.

Hussain, Zahid, "Pakistan Turns to Tribal Militias," *Wall Street Journal*, September 30, 2008, p. A13.

Jahanzeb, Miangul, and Fredrik Barth, *The Last Wali of Swat: An Autobiography*, Bangkok: Orchid Press, 2006.

Jihadist website, February 4, 2009. As of February 2009:
http://www.AlBoraq.info

Johnson, Thomas H., "Financing Afghan Terrorism: Thugs, Drugs, and Creative Movements of Money," in Giraldo and Trinkunas, eds., *Terrorism Financing and State Responses*, 2007.

Johnson, Thomas H., and M. Chris Mason, "Understanding the Taliban Insurgency in Afghanistan," *Orbis*, Vol. 51, No. 1, Winter 2007, pp. 71–89.

———, "No Sign Until the Burst of Fire: Understanding the Pakistan-Afghanistan Frontier," *International Security*, Vol. 32, No. 4, Spring 2008, pp. 41–77.

———, "All Counterinsurgency Is Local," *The Atlantic*, Vol. 302, No. 3, October 2008.

Jones, Seth G., *In the Graveyard of Empires: America's War in Afghanistan*, New York: W.W. Norton, 2009.

Kalyvas, Stathis N., *The Logic of Violence in Civil War*, New York: Cambridge University Press, 2006.

Karokhail, Masood, and Susanne Schmedil, *Integration of Traditional Structures into the State-Building Process: Lessons from the Tribal Liaison Office in Loya Paktia*, Kabul: Tribal Liaison Office, 2006.

Katz, David J., "Responses to Central Authority in Nuristan: The Case of the Vaygal Valley Kalasha," in Shahrani and Canfield, eds. *Revolutions and Rebellions in Afghanistan*, 1984.

Khalilzad, Zalmay, *Prospects for the Afghan Interim Government*, Santa Monica, Calif.: RAND Corporation, R-3949, 1991. As of April 8, 2010:
http://www.rand.org/pubs/reports/R3949/

Kilcullen, David, *The Accidental Guerrilla*, New York: Oxford University Press, 2009.

Kitson, Frank, *Low Intensity Operations: Subversion, Insurgency, Peacekeeping*, Hamden, Conn.: Archon Books, 1971.

———, *Bunch of Five*, London: Faber, 1977.

Klare, Michael T., and Peter Kornbluh, eds., *Low Intensity Warfare: Counterinsurgency, Proinsurgency, and Antiterrorism in the Eighties*, New York: Pantheon Books, 1988.

Krasner, Stephen D., *Sovereignty: Organized Hypocrisy*, Princeton, N.J.: Princeton University Press, 1999.

———, "Sharing Sovereignty: New Institutions for Collapsed and Failing States," *International Security*, Vol. 29, No. 2, Autumn 2004, pp. 85–120.

Kuntzsch, Feliz, *Afghanistan's Rocky Road to Modernity*, Québec: Université Laval, Institut Québécois des Hautes Études Internationales, July 2008.

Kuran, Timur, "New Out of Never: The Role of Surprise in the East European Revolution of 1989," *World Politics*, Vol. 44, No. 1, 1991, pp. 7–48.

Laitin, David D., *Identity in Formation: The Russian-Speaking Populations in the Near Abroad*, Ithaca, N.Y.: Cornell University Press, 1998.

Long, Austin, *On "Other War": Lessons from Five Decades of RAND Corporation Counterinsurgency Research*, Santa Monica, Calif.: RAND Corporation, MG-482-OSD, 2006. As of April 8, 2010:
http://www.rand.org/pubs/monographs/MG482/

Mao Tse-Tung, *On Guerrilla Warfare*, tr. Samuel B. Griffith II, Urbana, Ill.: University of Illinois Press, 1961.

Marten, Kimberly, "Warlordism in Comparative Perspective," *International Security*, Vol. 31, No. 3, Winter 2006–2007, pp. 41–73.

McChrystal, Stanley A., "COMISAF's Initial Assessment," memorandum to the Honorable Robert M. Gates, August 30, 2009.

McInerney, Michael, "The Battle for Deh Chopan, Part 1," *Soldier of Fortune*, August 2004.

———, "The Battle for Deh Chopan, Part 2," *Soldier of Fortune*, September 2004.

Methven, Stuart E., *Parapolitics and Pacification: A Study in Applied Cadre Techniques*, Cambridge, Mass.: Massachusetts Institute of Technology, Center for International Studies, 1967.

Miakhel, Shahmahmood, "The Importance of Tribal Structures and Pakhtunwali in Afghanistan: Their Role in Security and Governance," in Roy, ed., *Challenges and Dilemmas of State-Building in Afghanistan*, 2008, pp. 97–110.

Moghaddam, Sippi Azerbaijani, "Northern Exposure for the Taliban," in Giustozzi, ed., *Decoding the New Taliban*, 2009, pp. 57–59.

Motlaugh, Jason, "Pakistan's Use of Tribal Militias to Target Taliban Yields Mixed Results," *U.S. News & World Report*, December 5, 2008.

Nawaz, Shuja, *Crossed Swords: Pakistan, Its Army, and the Wars Within*, New York: Oxford University Press, 2008.

Nyrop, Richard F., and Donald M. Seekins, eds., "National Security," Afghanistan Country Study, Washington, D.C.: The American University, Foreign Area Studies, 1986.

Orr, Allan, "Recasting Afghan Strategy," *Small Wars and Insurgencies*, Vol. 20, No. 1, March 2009, pp. 87–117.

"Pakistan: Local Paramilitary Force to be Launched to Fight Taliban in NWFP," *The News Online* (Pakistan), May 28, 2009.

"Pakistan: Volunteer Forces Raised to Stop Militants from Entering Manshera, NWFP," *The News Online* (Pakistan), May 29, 2009.

Paris, Roland, *At War's End: Building Peace After Civil Conflict*, New York: Cambridge University Press, 2004.

Perlez, Jane, and Pir Zubair Shah, "Pakistan Uses Tribal Militias in Taliban War," *New York Times*, October 24, 2008.

Peters, Gretchen, *Seeds of Terror: How Heroin Is Bankrolling the Taliban and al Qaeda*, New York: St. Martin's Press, 2009.

Phillips, David, *Afghanistan: A History of Utilization of Tribal Auxiliaries*, Williamsburg, Va.: Tribal Analysis Center, 2008.

Philips, David L., White Paper Proposal Developed for Special Forces: Rural Development Team Project, McLean, Va.: Courage Services, 2009.

Quinlivan, James T., "Force Requirements in Security Operations," *Parameters*, Vol. 25, No. 4, Winter 1995–1996, pp. 59–69.

Ramin, Roohullah, "Afghanistan: Exploring the Dynamics of Sociopolitical Strife and Persistence of the Insurgency," Ottawa: Pearson Peacekeeping Centre, Occasional Paper 2, 2008.

Roe, A. M., "To Create a Stable Afghanistan: Provisional Reconstruction Teams, Good Governance, and a Splash of History," *Military Review*, Vol. 85, No. 6, 2005, pp. 20–26.

Roy, Arpita Basu, ed., *Challenges and Dilemmas of State-Building in Afghanistan: Report of a Study Trip to Kabul*, Delhi: Shipra Publications, 2008.

Roy, Olivier, *Islam and Resistance in Afghanistan*, 2nd ed., New York: Cambridge University Press, 1990.

Rubin, Barnett R., *The Fragmentation of Afghanistan: State Formation and Collapse in the International System*, 2nd ed., New Haven, Conn.: Yale University Press, 2002.

Ruttig, Thomas, "Loya Paktia's Insurgency: The Haqqani Network as an Autonomous Entity," in Giustozzi, ed., *Decoding the New Taliban*, 2009, pp. 57–101.

Schelling, Thomas, *Micromotives and Macrobehavior*, New York: Norton, 1978.

Schetter, Conrad, Raineer Glassner, and Massod Karokhail, *Understanding Local Violence, Security Arrangements in Kandahar, Kunduz and Paktia (Afghanistan)*, Bonn: University of Bonn, Center for Development Research, May 2006.

Schmeidl, Susanne, and Masood Karokhail, "The Role of Non-State Actors in 'Community-Based Policing': An Exploration of the Arbakai (Tribal Police) in South-Eastern Afghanistan," *Contemporary Security Policy*, Vol. 30, No. 2, August 2009, pp. 318–342.

Schofield, Julian, and Reeta Tremblay, "Why Pakistan Failed: Tribal Focoism in Kashmir," *Small Wars and Insurgencies*, Vol. 19, No. 1, March 2008, pp. 23–38.

Sedra, Mark, *Challenging the Warlord Culture: Security Sector Reform in Post-Taliban Afghanistan*, Bonn: Bonn International Center for Conversion, 2002.

Sen, Amartya, *Development as Freedom*, New York: Anchor Books, 2000.

Shahrani, M. Nazif, "Introduction: Marxist 'Revolution' and Islamic Resistance in Afghanistan," in Shahrani and Canfield, eds. *Revolutions and Rebellions in Afghanistan*, 1984, pp. 3–57.

Shahrani, M. Nazif, and Robert L. Canfield, eds., *Revolutions and Rebellions in Afghanistan: Anthropological Perspectives*, Berkeley, Calif.: Institute of International Studies, University of California, Berkeley, 1984.

Siegel, Daniel, and Joy Hackel, "El Salvador: Counterinsurgency Revisited," in Klare and Kornbluh, eds., *Low Intensity Warfare*, 1988.

Sinno, Abdulkader H., *Organizations at War in Afghanistan and Beyond*, Ithaca, N.Y.: Cornell University Press, 2008.

Strand, Richard F., "The Evolution of Anti-Communist Resistance in Eastern Nuristan," in Shahrani and Canfield, eds. *Revolutions and Rebellions in Afghanistan*, p. 91.

Stubbs, Richard, *Hearts and Minds in Guerrilla Warfare: The Malayan Emergency, 1948–1960*, New York: Oxford University Press, 1989.

Taliban Voice of Jihad Online, April 29, 2009.

Tapper, Richard, ed., *The Conflict of Tribe and State in Iran and Afghanistan*, New York: St. Martin's Press, 1983.

Tariq, Mohammed Osman, *Tribal Security System (Arbakai) in Southeast Afghanistan*, London: Crisis States Research Centre, December 2008.

Tierney, John J., Jr., *Chasing Ghosts: Unconventional Warfare in American History*, Washington, D.C.: Potomac Books, 2007.

Tribal Analysis Center, "The Panjpai Relationship with the Other Durranis," research paper, Williamsburg, Va., January 2009. As of April 9, 2010: http://www.tribalanalysiscenter.com/Research-Completed.html

―――, "The Quetta Shura: A Tribal Analysis," research paper, Williamsburg, Va., October 2009. As of April 9, 2010 http://www.tribalanalysiscenter.com/Research-Completed.html

Tribal Liaison Office, *Good Governance in Tribal Areas Kandahar Research Project: Research Report*, Kabul, 2005.

Trinquier, Roger, *Modern Warfare: A French View of Counterinsurgency*, trans. Daniel Lee, New York: Praeger, 2006.

U.S. Agency for International Development, *Tactical Conflict Assessment and Planning Framework*, Kabul, 2009.

U.S. Army Training and Doctrine Command, G2 Human Terrain System, *My Cousin's Enemy Is My Friend: A Study of Pashtun "Tribes,"* Fort Leavenworth, Kan.: United States Army, September 2009.

U.S. Army and U.S. Marine Corps, *Counterinsurgency*, FM 3-24, MCWP 3-33.5, Washington, D.C.: Headquarters Department of the Army and Headquarters Marine Corps Combat Development Command, December 2006.

———, *Counterinsurgency Field Manual*, Chicago: University of Chicago Press, 2007.

United Nations Security Council, Resolution 1267, New York, October 15, 1999.

Warren, Alan, "'Bullocks Treading Down Wasps'? The British Indian Army in Waziristan in the 1930s," *South Asia*, Vol. 19, No. 2, 1996, pp. 35–56.

World Bank, *Governance Matters, 2006: Worldwide Governance Indicators*, Washington, D.C.: World Bank, 2006.

Younossi, Obaid, Peter Dahl Thruelsen, Jonathan Vaccaro, Jerry M. Sollinger, and Brian Grady, *The Long March: Building an Afghan National Army*, Santa Monica, Calif.: RAND Corporation, MG-845-RDCC/OSD, 2009. As of April 8, 2010: http://www.rand.org/pubs/monographs/MG845/

Zaeef, Abdul Salam, *My Life with the Taliban*, New York: Hurst & Company, 2010.

Zahar, Marie-Joelle, "Proteges, Clients, Cannon Fodder: Civil-Militia Relations in Internal Conflicts," in Simon Chesterman, ed., *Civilians in War*, 2001, pp. 43–65.

Zisk, Kimberly Marten, *Enforcing the Peace: Learning from the Imperial Past*, New York: Columbia University Press, 2004.

Made in the USA
Lexington, KY
24 December 2011